D0889330

THE WESTERN FRONTIER LIBRARY

DISCARDED

DISCA. DED

BILL DOOLIN
Outlaw O. T.

BILL DOOLIN
OUTLAW O. T.

INGALLS, O.T., SEPTEMBER 1, 1893

COLONEL BAILEY C. HANES

With an Introduction by
RAMON F. ADAMS

UNIVERSITY OF OKLAHOMA PRESS : *NORMAN*

COLLEGE OF THE SEQUOIAS
LIBRARY

By Colonel Bailey C. Hanes

The Complete Bulldog (Richmond, Virginia, 1956)
The New Complete Bulldog (New York, 1966, 1973)
Bill Doolin, Outlaw O.T. (Norman, 1968, 1980)
Bill Pickett, Bulldogger: The Biography of a Black Cowboy (Norman, 1977)

International Standard Book Number: 0-8061-1652-8

Library of Congress Catalog Card Number: 68–15673

Copyright © 1968 by the University of Oklahoma Press, Norman, Publishing Division of the University. All rights reserved. Manufactured in the U.S.A. First edition, 1968. First paperback printing, 1980.

3   4   5   6   7   8   9   10   11   12

TO STEVEN MARK HANES

My Number Two Grandson

INTRODUCTION
by Ramon F. Adams

BILL DOOLIN was one of the most active outlaws in Oklahoma Territory and was known as "King of Oklahoma Outlaws." Yet until now there has never been a complete biography written about him.

True, many books and magazine articles have given scattered accounts of him, most of them unreliable. For instance, some reports have him dying of brain fever, but buckshot wounds are not a symptom of brain fever. Some have him killed in the daytime, but the event took place between eight and nine o'clock at night. Some have him killed from ambush when he went to keep an rendezvous with his wife, but when he was killed he had already been reunited with her and had loaded their scant household goods onto a wagon for a move to a new life. Most writers have him killed by Heck Thomas, but Thomas had a Winchester, and Doolin was killed with a shotgun.

One writer who has Doolin dying a natural death states: "They propped the dead body up against a tree and shot him full of holes. Took the body to Stillwater and had it photographed. . . . Noticed that he had not bled. . . . Everything was quieted down—the reward paid." Some said that Doolin's father-in-law did this deed to collect the reward for his daughter, but his father-in-law was a minister and a Christian man.

Besides, Doolin and his wife were devoted to each other, and Mrs. Doolin would never have allowed such a thing.

At the time of his death Doolin had risked capture to move his family to a faraway place where he could make a new start. He had told his wife that he was tired of outlaw life and of always being on the run and separated from his family. One wonders what kind of citizen he would have made if he had not been killed before he had a chance at a new start.

His short stay at Burden, Kansas, where he lived quietly with his family for a short time before he was captured at Eureka Springs, Arkansas, was the first peace he had known since his marriage, and he relished it. Suffering from arthritis and longing to live quietly with his family, he gave much thought to reforming and settling down. His friend Oscar Halsell urged him to surrender and stand trial, but Doolin knew that there were too many charges against him and that he was charged in the killing of three marshals at Ingalls, though Arkansas Tom had also been charged with the killings and had been convicted of shooting Marshal Hueston. Doolin told his wife that he had never knowingly killed a man.

Bill's father, Mack Doolin, was an Arkansas farmer with practically no education. Bill had no opportunity for education either, but he possessed an engaging personality, and in his young manhood he was a quiet fellow who avoided quarrels and, in spite of temptations, was not given to the heavy drinking so common among his companions. Because he was a farm boy and, unlike most cowboys, could use an ax, he was hired by rancher Oscar D. Halsell to help build a new ranch headquarters. After it was complete, Doolin worked to become an expert cowboy. Halsell was very fond of Bill and taught him to read and write well enough to keep a simple set of ranch books. Bill proved to be thoroughly honest and reliable, so much so that he was trusted to manage the ranch when Halsell was away.

Unfortunately, most of Halsell's other employees turned out to be outlaws in their spare time. From the Halsell ranch came most of the outlaws who rode with the Daltons and later with Doolin. Somewhere along the line Doolin's association with them won him over to "ridin' the high lines." It is my opinion that Doolin was a product of his time and environment and that under more favorable conditions he would not have followed the dim trails.

If his effort to move his family that fatal night had been successful, Doolin would probably have gone to New Mexico, where he had visited several times earlier. On one trip he had become acquainted with Eugene Manlove Rhodes, the noted writer. On one occasion, when Rhodes was trying to break a horse for him, Doolin shot the horse to keep the bronc from stomping Rhodes to death. After this incident each man felt that he had found a friend in the other. Later, in his novel *The Trusty Knaves*, Rhodes based a character named William Hawkins on Doolin.

Doolin told Rhodes that he was going to quit outlawry, bring his family to New Mexico, and settle down in the San Andres Mountains. He was killed fifteen months after he left the Rhodes ranch, and it was many months more before

Rhodes learned of it. Rhodes liked Doolin, as he did many other men outside the law, and when he heard of Doolin's death, he exclaimed, "What a waste!"

Though Doolin was uneducated, he had a natural gift for leadership. Like all cowboys, he knew horses, and he became an expert with guns. He was with the Daltons when they carried out their first train robbery at Redrock and doubtless learned much from them, but he proved to be a better leader. While the Dalton gang lasted only about fifteen months, the Doolin gang was active for about four years, largely because of Doolin's generalship. He planned every robbery carefully and saw to it that each member of his gang carried out his appointed duty effectively. Another reason for his success was that he knew every mile of Oklahoma Territory and all the places for a safe holdout, as well as the people who could be trusted. Under his leadership his hard-riding gang blazed a daring trail through the Indian Nation.

Until the Daltons planned the Coffeyville raid, which turned out to be a fiasco, he followed the Dalton brothers faithfully. But when Bob Dalton got so ambitious that he wanted to outdo the James gang and rob two banks simultaneously, Doolin, an older man with a cool head, thought the plan foolish and tried to talk him out of it. Dalton, elated with past successes, refused to listen.

Most historians claim that Doolin was absent from the Coffeyville raid only because his horse had gone lame, adding that by the time he had secured another horse and gone a few miles on his way to join the Daltons he met a rider from Coffeyville who told him of their failure and death. This story was evidently created by Richard S. Graves and related in his book *Oklahoma Outlaws* (1915, pages 53–54), and was repeated by such writers as Fred Sutton, in *Hands Up* (1927, pages 188–89); J. A. Newsom, in *The Life and Practice of the Wild and Modern Indian* (1923, pages 161–62); Everitt Dumas Nix, in *Oklahombres* (1929, page 46); Glenn Shirley, in *Six-Gun and Silver Star* (1955, pages 44–45); Zoe Tilghman, in *Outlaw Days* (1926); and Paul I. Wellman, in *Dynasty of Western Outlaws* (1961). I also accepted this legend and related it in *Burs Under the Saddle* before I learned the truth about the incident.

Colonel Hanes claims that Doolin had quit the Daltons before they made the Coffeyville raid. This seems logical; I do not believe that Doolin, levelheaded as he was, would have joined in such a foolhardy stunt, especially in a town where the Daltons were so well known. Bitter Creek Newcomb and Charlie Pearce quit the Daltons at the same time Doolin did.

Another often-told legend which Colonel Hanes rightly ignores in this biography is the one concerning the fight at Ingalls. Most writers claim that Rose of Cimarron was Bitter Creek's sweetheart. According to this version, when he was wounded by the first shot of the battle and was hiding behind a well on the street, Rose was in the upper story of Mrs. Pierce's hotel. She tied bedsheets together, slid down from the window, and took Bitter Creek his Winchester and ammunition. The true story is that Bitter Creek was on horseback on his way to see his girl friend, Sadie Conley, the widow of U.S. Marshal John Conley, when he was shot by Deputy Speed.

Wellman wrote that Bitter Creek went to the livery stable after he was wounded. He wrote of Rose of Cimarron: "Rose had seen her lover fall then scramble to the livery stable. She knew that his Winchester and cartridge belt were in his room on the second floor of the hotel at the rear of which she and the other woman were huddled. . . . She ran to the room and brought back the rifle and ammunition. The only possible regular exit from the second floor was exposed to the marshals' fire, so with Mary Pierce's help she tied the gun and belt in the corner of a sheet and lowered them to the ground from a window on the sheltered side of the building, then, tying two more sheets together, slid down herself."

Despite such legends, Rose of Cimarron was not in Ingalls that day, and Colonel Hanes correctly omits her from his detailed description of the fight.

This legend was another one perhaps started by Richard Graves, who, in his book *Oklahoma Outlaws* (pages 66–69), has Rose going through "a storm of bullets" to reach her sweetheart. The same story is repeated by Newsom, in *The Life and Practice of the Wild and Modern Indian* (pages 173–74); and by Zoe A. Tilghman, in *Outlaws Days* (pages 62–64). Other writers who repeated this tale are Edwin Sabin, in *Wild Men of the Wild West* (pages 314–15); Fred Sutton, in *Hands Up* (page 195); and James D. Horan, in *Desperate Women* (pages 204–205). Glenn Shirley, in *Toughest of Them All* (pages 117–30), also told this fable, though in a later book, *Six-Gun and Silver Star* (page 92), he was among the first to correct it.

To Doolin's credit, he was no killer. On many occasions he

could have killed, as when he escaped from the jail at Guthrie. In the battle at Ingalls he was shooting in self-defense. It was Arkansas Tom who killed Hueston, from an upstairs window of the Pierce Hotel. When one of the members of his gang, either Red Buck Weightman or Bitter Creek Newcomb, needlessly killed Preacher Godley, Doolin gave him a good cussing and broke up the gang.

After Doolin's death, Eugene Manlove Rhodes wrote to a friend: ". . . I have good reason to think that when he [Doolin] met Heck Thomas he was on his way back here, with his wife and child, to begin life afresh." Doolin was courageous and a devoted family man, and I agree with Rhodes that if he could have made his way back to New Mexico he would have become a good citizen. I can also echo Rhodes's comment, "What a waste!"

FOREWORD

This is the story of William "Bill" Doolin, one of the Southwest's most colorful and widely known outlaw chiefs. A full account of his life has never been attempted before. Most of the writings about Doolin have been concerned with some particular event or dealt with his contemporaries. This then, is as truthful and accurate an account as can be written, and it is based upon facts and evidence—carefully gathered, sifted, and evaluated—about a man, a territory, and the times.

Few men have led a more exciting life than this Oklahoma outlaw. As a legendary figure of our pioneer days, he has been credited with a multitude of deeds, some true and some not so true. I have sought to put things straight here.

I have attempted to make this account of Bill Doolin's life as complete and factual as exhaustive research, time and material will permit. Thus I have turned to books, newspaper files, printed articles, magazines, municipal records, memories of his contemporaries, and the verbal accounts of many people who knew him in one way or another. The result is, I think, as much information on Doolin as we're likely to discover.

Colonel Bailey C. Hanes

Santa Fe, New Mexico

ACKNOWLEDGMENT

To WHOM IT MAY CONCERN: I have read *Bill Doolin, Outlaw O. T.*, the biography of my late father, William "Bill" Doolin, by Colonel Bailey C. Hanes. I wish to state it is true, complete, and a factual picture of his life. For obvious reasons, much of the material has never before been published, so this is the first complete account to be written of my father and his gang of "outside the law" boys.

I would like to state that I have never been arrested for a crime, nor has any one of my children. This is not true of some of the Oklahoma Territory marshals. Although Bill Doolin was never praised for his law enforcement, he never had an outlaw son.

I want to endorse this biography personally, and I hope you, as a reader, will enjoy it as much as I have.

JAY DOOLIN (MEEK)

Ponca City, Oklahoma

CONTENTS

ILLUSTRATIONS

BILL DOOLIN
Outlaw O. T.

BILL DOOLIN: THE MAN
AND HIS BACKGROUND

BILL DOOLIN has become a legend in the history of the Southwest, especially Oklahoma. It was here that he made his headquarters and had his hideouts, rode the range as a cowboy and ranch foreman, married and fathered a son, and finally captained his own gang, made up of recruits from the remnants of former outlaw bands. And Doolin outshone them all.

It would be impossible to trace the life of Bill Doolin without a brief history of the Daltons, with whom he was associated in his early crimes of professional proportions.

James Lewis Dalton, Jr., was a Kentuckian, well respected and regarded as a good citizen. During the Mexican War in 1850, he served with the United States Army and after his discharge returned to Kentucky and engaged in farming and stock raising. He did a little horse trading on the side and took an active interest in racing.

Dalton soon moved to Missouri, however, where he lived for several years, at one time owning a saloon at Westport Landing. But, being a temperate man, he soon disposed of it. He built a large house near Kansas City—and he had need of it, for he became the father of fifteen children.

Dalton was not a vicious man, but was on the lazy side,

morose and gloomy. He loved good living, but he must also have possessed dormant hidden traits of instability that later cropped out in four of his sons.

Sixteen-year-old Adeline Younger became the bride of Lewis Dalton in 1851. She was an aunt of the infamous Youngers whose career in crime ended at the raid on the bank at Northfield, Minnesota. In 1860, Lewis and Adeline moved to Lawrence, Kansas, and later to Coffeyville, near the Indian Territory line. Mrs. Dalton, as mentioned, gave birth to fifteen children: five daughters and ten sons. Two, a girl and a boy, died in infancy. The remaining thirteen children grew up in the border country. Littleton and Charles drifted to Texas and Montana; William Marion (Bill) migrated to California, where he married and became interested in politics.

In 1862, Lewis, with the remainder of his family, moved to the Cherokee Nation. He leased land near Vinita, Indian Territory, until 1889, then made the run into Oklahoma Territory, but was unsuccessful in securing a claim. He returned to Coffeyville, where he worked at odd jobs until his death in 1890. Mrs. Dalton moved to Kingfisher, Oklahoma Territory, to live with her sons, Littleton, Charles, and Henry, who had returned to Oklahoma and obtained good farms. Three of the Dalton girls, Mamie, Eva, and Leona, married and located in the western part of the Territory. Frank Dalton, another son, became a deputy marshal, serving in 1884 under Isaac C. Parker, "the Hanging Judge," of Fort Smith, Arkansas. Regarded as a trustworthy and brave officer by Judge Parker, he was slain in 1887 in a gun battle west of Fort Smith while leading a posse and attempting to arrest some bootleggers in the Territory.

Gratton (Grat) Dalton was commissioned deputy marshal and took Frank's place. One of his first acts was to commission his brother Robert (Bob) as a posseman under his command. Emmett, still a boy of 17, was at this time working on the Bar X Bar Ranch with Bill Doolin and some of the other cowboys who were to make outlaw history in the 1890s. Emmett was never a federal officer, but when Bob was hired as chief of the Indian police force, Grat was also hired and Emmett served as a posseman. In 1889 and 1890, the Daltons headquartered at Pawhuska. Grat took a bribe and was discharged, Bob resigned as chief of police, Grat and Emmett refused wages offered them, and all three left the police force at the same time.

Thoroughly disgusted and resentful toward the laws they had sworn to uphold, they drifted west into New Mexico. One night while Grat, Emmett, Bob, George Newcomb, Charley Bryant, and Bill McElheney were gambling in a mining town saloon, an argument arose about the faro dealer being crooked and there was gunplay. They robbed the faro game and made an easy escape, pursued by officers and a posse of Mexicans. They were forced into a fight, killed several of the horses ridden by the Mexican possemen, but escaped unhurt. Riding hard, the boys returned to Indian Territory. Word got out that the Daltons had gone bad.

The three of them went to Fort Smith, where they stayed for a while before moving on to Claremore, remaining there until 1891. Then they made a trip to the Osage country and stole seventeen head of ponies and five pairs of mules. They took the stock to Wagoner, where they tried to sell to local buyers. Unable to make any trades, they drove the stolen animals toward Kansas. They traded the mules to Emmett Van in the Cherokee Nation and took the ponies into Kansas, where they were sold.

The Daltons next showed up in the neighborhood of Claremore and boldly rounded up and drove away about twenty-five or thirty head of horses belonging to Bob Rogers, Frank Musgrove, and other citizens. They sold the stock at Columbus, Kansas, to a horse trader by the name of Scott, using as references the names of some of the best men in the Territory. Scott gave them a check for $700, which they cashed, endorsing it with their proper names. Scott took the horses to a pasture near Baxter Springs, where their owners later found them.

Meanwhile, the boys had gathered up a second bunch of horses and on the very same day that Rogers and others were at Baxter Springs to recover their stolen property, Bob and Emmett arrived with the second herd. A posse was hurriedly formed to capture them, but they saddled fresh horses out of the stolen herd and lit out, with the posse in hot pursuit.

Emmett's horse gave out, and, meeting a man driving a team, they took his best horse, leaving with him the jaded steed and Emmett's saddle, bridle, and coat, which was tied behind the saddle. They were so hard pressed they didn't have time to transfer the saddle to the new horse. To make things worse, Grat was arrested while taking them fresh horses. Grat was lodged in the federal jail in Fort Smith, remaining there several weeks. Emmett and Bob escaped to California, where Bill Dalton was living. There was no evidence to implicate Grat in the horse-stealing business with his brothers, so he was released and also went to California.

In California, the four brothers were accused of robbing a Southern Pacific train on February 6, 1891. The express messenger resisted, and in the exchange of shots the fireman was wounded and died. The next day, Emmett, Grat, and Bill McElheney made their escape and split up. Some months later, however, they were together again in Indian Territory, where they hid out in the Turkey Track neighborhood on the Sac and Fox Indian Reservation. They drifted around, finding plenty of shelter among their old friends but carefully avoiding territorial law officers. All this time they talked of robbing a train, making plans to stage a train robbery just as soon as they could assemble a dependable gang for this purpose.

In the meantime, Grat, captured at his brother Bill's home, was tried for the Tulare County train robbery. He received a twenty-year sentence for his alleged part in the robbery. Bill, also charged in the raid, was acquitted as having no part in the crime. Grat escaped from his guards on the way to prison and headed for Oklahoma Territory. Bill sent word to Bob that Grat and McElheney were on their way home and to meet them with horses at Dover, Oklahoma Territory.

Bob had not been idle. He had visited ranches in the Triangle area, persuading certain cowboys to join him in carrying out plans he had carefully worked out during the past few months. In the new gang were Charley Bryant, Bill

7

McElheney, Charlie Pierce, Dick Broadwell, Bill Powers, George Newcomb, Bill Doolin, and, of course, Emmett, Grat, and Bob Dalton. Of these ten men, you have already met Bob, Grat, and Emmett. Bill Doolin was destined to become more widely known and much more successful in his outlawry than the Daltons ever were. More men were added from time to time, but usually not all were included in any one job.

A stalwart in the gang was "Black-Faced" Charley Bryant, who was born in a log cabin in Wise County, Texas. He had an ugly black scar on one side of his face where a bullet from a cowboy's exploding gun, discharged close to him in a gunfight, had creased his cheek. Burned black powder, imbedded beneath the skin around the wound, made the splotch which gave him his nickname. Charley was a slender man, small and insignificant in appearance, but he had few superiors outside the law in the West. He was a splendid rider, a good shot, and a man to be relied upon. Visits to "red lights" had required more and more of his money and cowpunching failed to yield enough, so he became an outlaw.

William (Bill) McElheney, the "Narrow-Gauged Kid," was a close friend of Grat Dalton. He was originally from Arkansas, where he returned to his sister's home in 1891 and never rejoined the Dalton gang. However, he was with the Daltons on their trip to New Mexico and took part in the saloon holdup and gunfight there. When he returned from Arkansas, he was active in the Ingalls area. After the Coffeyville affair, he stole cattle and rode a few times with Doolin.

Charlie Pierce, a Texan, first settled in Pawnee, Oklahoma

Territory. He was known in the Territory as a "race horse man" who brought two running horses with him from Texas. He had a wild nature, with nerve and courage that made him an ideal prospect for an outlaw. Charlie was a close friend of George Newcomb and finally died by the latter's side near Ingalls, Oklahoma Territory, on the Dunn farm.

Bill Powers, alias Tom Evans, alias Joe Evans, was regarded by the Daltons as a good man and was present on most of their jobs. He was probably born in Texas. For a time, Bill was wagon boss for the Hashknife Ranch on the Pecos. He was finally laid off and drifted to Oklahoma, probably with a trail herd. He worked for O. D. Halsell on the HH Ranch before the opening of Oklahoma Territory in 1889 and his subsequent joining up with the Daltons.

Richard L. (Dick) Broadwell, "Texas Jack" started out as a horse thief but soon graduated to bigger things. He was another Texas cowboy who had come up the trail with a cattle herd. A Halsell rider, Dick was acquainted with most of the men he was later to be associated with in crime.

Handsome George Newcomb, known as "Bitter Creek," and "Slaughter's Kid," came from a good Fort Scott, Kansas, family. He ran away from home in the 1880s and went to Texas, where he became a cowboy. He worked for Colonel C. J. Slaughter at the Long S Ranch on the headwaters of the Colorado River. It was while working for Slaughter that he was dubbed "Slaughter's Kid." He finally went up the trail and located in the Cherokee Strip, where he worked for the 4D outfit and later for the Bar X Bar, Turkey Track, and

HH ranches. Newcomb had a claim near Guthrie, Oklahoma Territory, where he lived for a time prior to beginning his first association with the new Dalton gang. He was in New Mexico with the Daltons.

Emmett Dalton and Charley Bryant met Grat Dalton and Bill McElheney at Dover with fresh horses and new Winchesters. The trip from California on horseback had taken 110 days. That night, the four men rode on down to Newcomb's homestead near Guthrie. The next morning, Newcomb joined them on their trek to the wilds of the South Canadian River and Jim Riley's ranch. At Guthrie, McElheney left the group and went to Arkansas to visit his sister.

Big Jim Riley was a stage driver between Fort Reno and Caldwell, Kansas, before he married a Cheyenne Indian woman and settled down to ranching and harboring outlaws. He was well to do and was never accused of taking part in any of the robberies committed by his guests. At his ranch, Emmett, Grat, Bryant, and Newcomb joined Bill Doolin, Dick Broadwell, and Bill Powers, who were camped and waiting for them. These men, together with Charlie Pierce, were positively the only men ever connected in any way with Bob Dalton's gang and its lawless enterprises.

Barton Doolin was born about 1784 in Kentucky of good pioneer stock. He married a young Kentucky woman of similar background whose Christian name was Elizabeth, family name unknown. To this union were born several children, the only one of whom we have a record being Michael. He was also born in Kentucky, probably in January or February, 1805. Michael—Mack for short—grew to manhood in his native state and was married to Mary of the Rubettom and Cooksey families, who went to California at an early date, probably about 1831. Shortly after their marriage, Michael and Mary moved to Missouri, where their first son, Barton, was born in 1832.

Between the years 1832 and 1838, the couple moved to Newton County, Arkansas. In the meantime, Barton and Elizabeth Doolin moved from Kentucky to Johnson County, adjoining Newton on the south, where Michael had settled. While living in Newton County, Mary gave birth to four children: Telitha, a daughter born in 1837; Jamima, a second daughter born in 1840; John, born in 1845; and Mary, a third daughter, born in 1848.

Sometime around 1850, Mary Doolin died, and Michael moved with his four children to his parents' farm in northeast Johnson County. There he met and fell in love with a young woman by the name of Artemina Beller, whom he married on January 17, 1856. She was 36 and he 50 at the time. They had two children: William (Bill), in 1858, and Tennessee, a daughter, in 1859. These are the only children of Artemina found in the records; however, Mary's children still lived with their father and stepmother.

Until 1860, Michael sharecropped in Johnson County. That year he bought a beautiful, improved forty-acre farm (NE¼, Section 28, Township 12 North, Range 21 West). It was located twenty-five miles up the Big Piney River north of the Arkansas River and thirty-five miles north and a little east of the county seat, Clarksville, in the township of Pilot Rock. The farm was surrounded by high peaks of the

Ozarks, guarded by large trees and high mountains on three sides. The land was level and the soil fertile. With the cold, clear water of the Big Piney on the south, it was a place of abundance and beauty. There were large rocks and big bass in the river, so fishing was good—and the mountain streams never failed.

Here in this beautiful spot Mack made his home, fenced his property with a native stone fence, and reared his family. Located a short distance west of the Doolin farm was Fort Douglas, established by the United States Army when it drove the Cherokee Indians into Oklahoma Territory. The site of the fort was at one time the capital of the Cherokee Nation West, which may well have been the Indian town visited by Hernando de Soto after he left Hot Springs during his exploration in Arkansas.

Before the Civil War, the owners of the land in this section were considered "good livers," and some owned slaves. They had cattle and hogs, and the climate was so mild that they were able to raise two gardens a year, in spring and fall, as well as corn and wheat. There were water mills nearby to grind their grain. Five different varieties of nuts were to be had for the picking, along with wild strawberries, grapes, blackberries, dewberries, cherries, apples, and peaches. There was plenty of deer for meat, cotton and wool for the housewife to card and spin, and feathers for beds were abundant.

In 1833, Hugh Gilbert owned a grist mill on the Big Piney. In the same year, General Albert Pike was living with Abraham Smith in the vicinity, teaching at a school on the Big Piney. Steamboats took the place of the old keelboats on the

Arkansas River as early as 1835, going as far west as Fort Gibson and south to New Orleans. It was in these beautiful and happy surroundings that young Bill Doolin spent his formative years.

In February, 1863, John, half-brother of Bill Doolin, went to Fayetteville and enlisted as a private in the Union Army, Company C, First Regiment, Arkansas Infantry Volunteers. His commanding officer was Colonel James M. Johnson. John's military record reveals that he was born in Newton County, Arkansas, and was eighteen years of age when he enlisted on February 12, 1863, for a term of three years. He was five feet in height, with fair skin, hazel eyes, and dark hair. Occupation: farmer. He mustered in at Fayetteville on February 27, 1863; was absent without leave on January 29, 1864; absent, sick, at Fort Smith, March 24, 1864; absent by arrest at Fort Smith, April 17, 1864. He was sentenced to military prison at Alton, Illinois, for two years at hard labor, with loss of pay and allowances, by order of a general court-martial under terms of General Order No. 45, Frontier District, Fort Smith, Arkansas, September 30, 1864. He was confined at Fort Smith until March 3, 1865, at which time he escaped his guards. His name was placed on the list of deserters and a bounty offered for his capture. But he was never recaptured or returned to prison, and when his regiment was mustered out August 10, he was still missing.

Michael Doolin died in 1865, shortly after John's escape from prison at Fort Smith, and John subsequently returned home to the farm. Artemina, with her children, William and Tennessee, and her stepson John, remained on the farm for several years. During this time, Bill Doolin learned to use his rifle well and became an expert in making fence posts, cutting firewood, and hewing building logs with an ax and saw from timber on the farm.

William Doolin was a quiet man, never given to quarreling or heavy drinking. He was a leader of men, for he had a commanding, magnetic personality. These qualities made up in a great measure for his lack of formal education and family background. He was tall—six feet, two inches, to be exact—strikingly slender, weighing 150 pounds, with thick, unruly auburn hair, often mentioned as being "all but black," above a high forehead. Penetrating pale-blue eyes, thin lips, and canine teeth were his trademark. And his nose was long and thin, with a pronounced hook at the end. He always wore a ragged brindled moustache that practically covered his straight mouth. Once seen, his facial features were said never to be forgotten.

Bill Doolin was twenty-three years old in 1881 when he decided to go west, for stories of free land and great opportunities to be had there were upon the lips of everyone he met. He first went to Fort Smith, where he spent a few days and finally signed on as a helper with a freight outfit headed for Caldwell, Kansas, on the frontier. His first job out of Caldwell seems to have been with the Three Circle Ranch, with headquarters on the north bank of the Cimarron River five miles northeast of present-day Guthrie, Oklahoma. He was back in Caldwell a second time in 1882.

When Doolin arrived in Caldwell, he began looking for another job. It so happened that Oscar D. Halsell, a Texas rancher, was in town gambling for a stake to buy provisions for his new ranch in the Indian country. Doolin and Halsell met, and the rancher took a liking to the slim young man from Arkansas. Halsell was looking for someone who could use an ax—and few cowboys could—in constructing corrals and buildings at his ranch in the lush Cowboy Flats area of what is now Logan County, Oklahoma.

Halsell's cowboys were no good with an ax, but Doolin filled the bill. He was young, energetic, and an expert with both ax and saw, so Halsell hired him. The next day, Doolin and Halsell returned to the ranch. They immediately cut out Halsell's cattle from the Wyeth herd, where they had been left temporarily, and cut off range on which to run them. There were now more than 500 head of cattle in the Halsell holdings, besides ten good saddle horses and a year's grubstake.

There was no town of Guthrie, nor any other town in the entire Territory, in 1882—just Indians, cowboys, cattle, horses, and an abundance of wild game. Indian Territory was unsettled all the way from Kansas on the north to the Red River on the south, a distance of 250 miles. It was lush prairie country, with ample water in many creeks and rivers. And there was shade along the streams. In summer it was a cattle paradise with an oversupply of fine native grasses.

Five miles north of the present city of Guthrie, the course of the Cimarron River runs east for about a mile, then almost north for four miles, then southeast for two miles. From this spot, until the river reaches the Arkansas, its course is nearly due east. South of a bend in the river thirteen miles east of Guthrie is a beautiful valley comprising 10,000 acres of fine native grass-land, named "Cowboy Flats" by the ranchers. In this valley, running ten miles south and reaching into the scattered post-oak and blackjack timber, was the site of Oscar Halsell's new ranch, the HH. Oscar's brother, H. H. Halsell, also ran cattle on the ranch from time to time. His brand was $\frac{H\ H}{H}$.

Doolin and other cowboys set to work building the ranch headquarters. At this time, Halsell's crew was made up of Mat Laughlin, Dick West, Zin Fitzgerald, sixteen-year-old Furd Halsell, Doolin, Oscar Halsell, H. H. Halsell, and Nigger Amos, the ranch cook. They selected two sandhills facing each other, with a space of sixteen feet separating them. A large dugout was built in each hill, one dugout facing the other, forming two 16x20 foot rooms. A roofed breezeway between them made a cool and convenient place for the ranch hands to eat their meals. Bill Doolin sealed the two dugout rooms with split cedar logs, thus making them pleasant-smelling living quarters the year round.

Bill liked the new cowboy life; he was a willing worker and soon became a top hand on the Halsell spread. He could not read or write when he went to work at the ranch, but Halsell soon taught him to read and to keep simple ranch books. As time passed, Doolin assumed more and more of the responsibilities of the ranch; he kept the books and was in charge when the Halsells were away, for he was consid-ered completely trustworthy. He took cowboys to Caldwell and bought supplies for the ranch and held many positions while in Halsell's employ. Doolin's several bosses and the cowboys who worked with him said they had never known a more likable man.

It was while Doolin was working on the HH Ranch for Halsell that he became acquainted with most of the cowboys who later became territorial outlaws and belonged to his gang or Dalton's wild bunch. Little Dick West, Emmett Dalton, Bitter Creek Newcomb, Bill Raidler, Dick Broadwell and Bill Powers were the most notorious, most talked about. They were all cowboys on the HH, and all rode guard and stood night watch with Doolin at one time or another.

The winter of 1882–83 was a very hard one, and many cattle were lost. The remaining Halsell cattle were rounded up in the summer of 1883 and shipped to market in Chicago. Late the same summer, H. H. Halsell went to Texas to pick up a trail herd of Texas cattle to restock the Halsell ranch. As trail hands, he took with him Doolin, West, and one or two others. This was Doolin's first trip to the Lone Star State.

Doolin worked off and on for the Halsell brothers from 1882 until the early 1890s. He also worked for most of the other cow outfits in the Territory at one time or another. He was second boss, and later foreman, on the old Bar X Bar Ranch for several years. Owned by Ed Hewins and Milt Bennett, it was located in the Triangle country, the Cherokee land bounded on the north and east by the Arkansas River and on the south and east by the Cimarron, with the third side abutting the Pawnee Reservation on the west. Within these boundaries were 105,456 acres of leased good and bad land where the Bar X Bar ran 10,000 head of cattle.

Bill Doolin named Hell Roaring Creek, three miles from Blackburn, while he worked for the Bar X Bar. Doolin and a bunch of cowboys were bedded down on a ranch near the creek one night. It had been raining hard, but the tired punchers slept peacefully near the creek bed. Finally, one of them awakened to find a wet bedroll and the creek running out of its banks. "Bill, get up," he yelled. "The creek is high!" Doolin took one startled, half-awake look and said: "Yes, it's hell roaring high!" The name stuck, and the creek became known as Hell Roaring Creek.

The roster of cowboys who worked at the ranch reads like a *Who's Who of Outlaws, 1880–1900,* for they included Bill Doolin, Tulsa Jack Blake, Bitter Creek Newcomb, Charlie Pierce, and Emmett Dalton. The ranchers were not outlaws, but the ranch, located far down the Cimarron in a remote and generally unknown area, was for years a favorite hangout of horse thieves and other criminals.

The Baker gang was the first to learn of the hideout and the safety it offered them in the caves and forests of the Triangle. Baker Cave, near Keystone, is a monument to them. The Bakers were Cherokee citizens who served in the Confederate Army and turned outlaw after the Civil War. Baker was wounded and captured in the Triangle and hauled in a spring wagon to Coffeyville, Kansas, where a reward for his capture was paid. He died of wounds shortly after being identified and turned over to law officers.

It was in the spring of 1880, while working for the Bar X Bar, that Bill McGinty, early-day cowboy and champion bronc rider, became acquainted with Bill Doolin when

Doolin and some other Bar X Bar hands were unloading cattle at the Santa Fe Railroad's Red Rock Station on the Oto Indian Reservation. The ranch was on Cherokee land and not subject to the 1889 run, but was opened for settlement in 1893. Doolin worked here after the opening of Oklahoma Territory in 1889.

Doolin and Newcomb also worked for the Turkey Track Ranch for a time. This ranch was located on Sac and Fox land and joined the Bar X Bar range on the south, separated from it only by the Cimarron River. The ranch was a hideout and a place of employment for many outlaws. Doolin was also a hand on the old H.D. spread, owned by a man named Freeman and located near where the town of Hominy is now situated. The trading center was Arkansas City, Kansas.

Doolin was employed by T. H. Hill of Arkansas City in the fall of 1888 and worked cattle for the Wyeth Cattle Company on the Salt Fork River in Indian Territory. He ran with the H.D. crowd, and Hill said he was the most peaceful and quiet man in the whole outfit. The H.D. bunch made a specialty of going to Arkansas City periodically and attempting to run the town. They were not usually successful in taking over completely, but they did paint her a bright red. Doolin seldom accompanied the gang to town on a spree. Another rider for Hill at this time was Bitter Creek Newcomb, who was noted for his presence at dances far and near.

One Fourth of July while Doolin was employed at the Bar X Bar, a group of cowboys rode off to Coffeyville, Kansas, for a three-day celebration. Things were a little dull, so Doolin and his cronies decided to have a celebration on their own. They borrowed some ash barrels that had been sawed in two in the middle and filled them with ice and bottled beer. They also bought two kegs of cold beer. All this was hauled up into the timber about a quarter of a mile from town and set up for distribution so all could have their fill while they talked, told tall tales, and smoked under the shade of the trees.

About the middle of the afternoon, a couple of deputy sheriffs came out from town and asked who owned the beer. Bill Doolin was always the spokesman for his crowd, and they waited for him to answer. He said, "Why, the beer doesn't belong to anybody! It's free, gentlemen, help yourselves!"

The officers replied that if they could not find the owner, they would have to confiscate the beer, since Kansas was a dry state and beer was illegal. The deputy began to roll a keg of beer away, and a gunfight started. Both deputies were shot. Who fired the shots was never determined, but since Doolin was the leader, he was held responsible. From that day on, he was on the dodge in the state of Kansas.

2

BILL DOOLIN SIDESWIPES THE LAW

To SAY THAT BILL DOOLIN was an outlaw by choice alone is not true, but to say that he could have been otherwise might also be untrue. He was a product of his time and environment, with no excuse for his profession other than the fact that circumstances dealt him a hand in life which destiny, and even necessity, as well as habit, helped him to play. One must keep in mind that he lived out his life in a wild, raw, rugged new country, surrounded generally by coarse, desperate, rough, and violent men in a society where violence was an accepted way of life. During his picturesque life, he made many friends—and many enemies.

Bill Doolin was not a wizard of the quick draw, but he was a calm, deliberate, deadly accurate shot with either revolver or rifle. It was his habit to practice much with each, both on foot and on the back of a running horse. His chief stock in trade was his knowledge of the country, expert marksmanship, and dexterity with his gun. He required as much of each member of his gang throughout the years. He was considered by the members of his gang, as well as by U.S. marshals and sheriffs, as a true shot who almost never missed his target, whether it was moving or stationary, whether he was mounted or on foot.

Doolin was regarded by the U.S. marshals in Guthrie,

Oklahoma Territory, as a cool, desperate, dangerous man not likely to be taken alive. Marshals on several occasions, however, pointed out that he was not a bloodthirsty killer, but a man who on more than one occasion restrained his gang from senseless killings and violence, which he would not tolerate. Not a wanton killer, Doolin was always shrewd, fearless, and lawless.

Although Bill Doolin was an outlaw, he probably contributed more than any other single man to bringing law and order to the Territory. His crimes occurred so frequently and were so efficient that he could no longer be tolerated to run at large, and a mighty effort on the part of express companies, railroads, and the federal government wrote *finis* to his long, productive, and colorful career as "the king of the Oklahoma outlaws."

In Oklahoma, Kansas, Arkansas, and New Mexico, Doolin was accused of many crimes, including bank and train robbery, peddling whisky to the Indians, cattle and horse theft, and murder. It is interesting to note that he was never convicted of a single crime; he never spent a single day in jail, except upon the one occasion when Bill Tilghman brought him in on a warrant from Eureka Springs, Arkansas. This period, while he awaited trial, was a scant six months. Then he broke jail and was off again, never to return to a jail cell. In the latter part of his life, Doolin was the object of a $5,000 reward—dead or alive—which finally laid him low.

A large number of men contributed, each in his own way, to the growing reputation of Bill Doolin. At his door was laid the credit for many unsolved crimes in the Territory. He was accused of crimes committed while he was in jail, or when he was several hundred miles away, and even after his death he was popular with the press, which gave him an unearned reputation all over the Southwest.

Bill Doolin, like many other early-day cowboys in Indian Territory, sold whisky to restricted Indians. An Indian would pay any price or trade anything he might happen to own for the white man's firewater, which did such wonderful things for him. Cowboys and others had access to whisky, and it was a very profitable sideline at a time when money was very hard to come by and a cowboy's wages were meager at best. Doolin was known to be an offender by the U.S. marshals. Suspicion against a man and proof of his guilt, however, were quite different matters. A warrant was issued for Doolin's arrest, but it was never served.

On one occasion, Doolin was surrounded by a posse under the leadership of Deputy Sheriff Calvin Miller, who was searching for him but was not acquainted with him. This happened east of Braggs, in eastern Oklahoma Territory. Doolin started to resist arrest, but when he saw that he was surrounded by many guns, he surrendered instead. Miller questioned him about his identity, but since he had never seen Doolin before, he was unaware that he had the prize within his grasp. Doolin told Miller that he was a cowboy, that his name was Tom Wilson, and that he was employed by the Bar X Bar Ranch and was on his way home after taking care of some ranch business for the foreman. After some conversation, Miller was finally convinced he had the wrong man and let Doolin go.

For a while Doolin was on the payroll of the Open A cow outfit in the Territory. Finally, the urge to see the world seized him and he drifted up into the Wyoming cattle country and worked as a cowboy for the old XL Ranch for a time. Later he went to Montana and finally to California. After seeing the known cattle world of the West, he decided to go back to the Territory and his old saddle buddies. He gradually worked his way across Arizona and New Mexico. While in this area, he noted the extensive value of the locality as a hideout, if one ever had a need for such a place. It seemed that a man could become lost here forever if he so desired. Doolin then made his way across West Texas and back again into Indian Territory, where he hired out once more on the Bar X Bar. He also took up his old trade of peddling whisky to the Pawnee and Osage Indians.

Doolin had gone to work for the Halsells in the fall of 1888 at the HH Ranch. Then came the order from the U.S. government for the ranchers to vacate the land, for it was to be opened for homesteading in April, 1889. After the ranch was closed out in the fall and early spring, Doolin went to work again for the Bar X Bar, located in the Cherokee area, which would not be opened for settlement by homesteaders until 1893. While Doolin worked for Halsell, Bob Dalton made a special trip to propose that Doolin become a member of his gang of highwaymen and cattle thieves. He also hinted that there were greater things to come. Most of the territorial outlaws of that day worked at a regular job, made periodic raids, and returned to the ranches to hide out and thus hold down suspicion. So Doolin, like the rest, robbed and worked alternately throughout his career.

Rolla Goodnight worked for a number of years at the KKK Cattle Company ranch twenty miles southeast of Arkansas City. He knew Bill Doolin well and was also acquainted with Bill's half-brother John, who had come to Oklahoma Territory from Arkansas to work on a ranch with Bill. During the early 1890s, the Doolins would stop at the ranch for a night's lodging or a meal with Rolla and his wife on their way to and from Arkansas City and the Territory. The Goodnights reported that the boys were always polite and paid for their meals and horse feed before leaving.

John finally settled in the Oilton area. There is no indication that he was ever an outlaw. Phil Traband of Guthrie reported that in 1914, while he was deputy sheriff of Logan County, he went to Oilton to pick up a prisoner and the marshal who delivered the prisoner was Walter Doolin. Phil asked if he was related to the notorious outlaw, Bill Doolin, and was told that Bill was his uncle.

Bill Doolin worked for a while during 1890–91 in Guthrie at the Halsell Livery Stable, owned by O. D. Halsell. It was located on Oklahoma Avenue near Broad Street, next to Adam Traband's cigar factory. While working here, Doolin learned to enjoy Traband's fine handmade cigars, which Doolin bought by the box. The two men became very good friends. While working at the livery stable, Doolin became acquainted with Tom Dooley, another former cowboy, also on the payroll at the barn.

Kid was a pacer owned by Adam Traband, who loved to hitch him up to a sulky and dash up and down Broad Street. One night Kid was stolen from the barn on the alley. Quite disturbed, Adam told Bill Doolin of the theft on the following day. Doolin reassured him and said not to worry about it. Two mornings later, when Adam went to the barn, Kid was again in his stall.

Doolin and Dooley were hired to break raw, wild horses being brought in from Montana and other western states. They were hitched up and driven just enough to say that they had been worked. Some of the better quality horses were broken to the saddle and sold for cow ponies. It is believed that many horses stolen in the Territory passed through this barn in Guthrie, where they were slicked up or dyed a different color and taken to Perry. There they were sold to the army remount officer, loaded into railroad cars, and shipped out of the Territory to various cavalry stations in the West.

One evening, Dooley got into an argument with a Negro stable hand who was helping him clip a horse. The result was that Dooley cursed the Negro, who, in turn, threw a clipper head at Dooley. He then ran out the front door and south across Oklahoma Avenue, heading for a corn patch on the corner of Broad and Oklahoma Avenue where the Town House Motel is now located. Just as he made it to the first row of corn, Dooley drew his revolver and fired, but the Negro disappeared into the corn patch. Dooley saddled his horse, packed his gear in the bunkhouse, said good-bye to Doolin, mounted, and rode east out of town. He was never seen in the Territory again.

After Dooley's departure, a man with a lantern, at the insistence of Phil Traband, young son of Adam Traband, who had witnessed the shooting, found the Negro dead, with a bullet hole in his back, only a few rows out in the corn patch. Since no one signed a complaint and Dooley had already escaped for parts unknown, nothing was ever done about the shooting.

Bill Doolin was well acquainted in Guthrie, for he knew many former cowboys, as well as a number of other persons who had opened businesses in town. He was a frequent guest at the saloons and gambling houses, but he was a light drinker and moderate gambler, which was not true of his cronies. Incidentally, it was no problem to find a saloon in Guthrie in those days, for there were twenty-seven such places where you could quench your thirst, gamble away your money, or get in touch with a man who just might happen to know a lonesome woman for you. All this and the territorial capital, too!

While he was a cowhand for the Bar X Bar and the Turkey Track outfits and after the opening of Oklahoma Territory for settlement, Bill Doolin and other cowboys from various ranches in the flat-iron country began to spend a lot of time in the small, prosperous, and growing town of Ingalls, isolated in a remote corner of the county near the Creek Nation. The town was first established shortly after the run of 1889, and its first official post office opened on January 22, 1890, with Robert T. McCurty as postmaster. It had no railroads or main-traveled roads or even trails. But in spite of its remoteness, it continued to grow, and for some time the town of Ingalls was larger than the county seat of Stillwater.

The townsite of Ingalls was located in the northeast part of Payne County about four miles west of the territorial line, eleven miles east of Stillwater, and thirty-five miles northeast of Guthrie. It was believed that Ingalls would one day be the best town in Oklahoma Territory. Robert Beal, a farmer, and Dr. R. F. McCurty released from their original quarter-section homesteads forty acres to be used as a townsite for Ingalls. Later, in 1889, the U.S. government made the original survey and platted the town that same year. Beal established the first grocery store, and A. J. Light opened a blacksmith shop on the northwest corner of the townsite, where the road entered Ingalls from the west. On the adjoining lot to the south was the Pierce and Hostetler O.K. Livery Barn, and farther south, in the same block on the west side of the street, were a harness and saddle shop, Dr. McCurty's drugstore (in a frame building he had put up on one of the corners of the street), Bradley's general store, Perry's dry goods store, and Ramsey's hardware store.

On the opposite side of the street were Wagoner's blacksmith shop and Charley Vaughn's saloon. Here also was located a small dwelling, the Pierce O.K. Hotel, the only two-story building in town. On the south was located a drugstore owned by a man named Briggs. Across Second Street, (still on the west side of Ash Street), on the corner, was the George Ransom's saloon, and next door was a livery stable also owned by Ransom. South from First Street on Ash, but on the east side of the street, were the Ketchum Shoe Shop, then Charley Vaughn's saloon, and around the corner to the east on Second Street was the Nix Restaurant. South of Second on Ash were the post office and a few homes and other business buildings. Scattered about the townsite were a grist mill, a cotton gin, feed store, another restaurant, and a butcher shop, as well as a few other small establishments.

The post office changed hands, and J. W. Ellsworth, a preacher and notary public who had come to Ingalls from Iowa via Missouri with his family, became postmaster for about six months. He was succeeded by William Selph, who also put up a building and opened a grocery store. The post office was located there for quite some time before a building to house the post office was constructed.

The town boasted five doctors: J. H. Pickering, W. R. Call, D. H. Selph, R. F. McCurty, and a Dr. Briggs.

After serving as postmaster, Ellsworth moved his family to what is now Quay, several miles to the east and just over the line in Pawnee County. There he opened a general store and post office serving as postmaster several years. Tom Lawson married Lottie Ellsworth, the sister of Edith Doolin, and the town was named Lawson after him by his father-in-law, Ellsworth.

While a water well as being drilled in Ingalls, it was presumed that the drill struck a vein of coal. The news spread like prairie dust before the wind, and the citizens visualized their new town as the center of a coal mining district. A small amount of coal was found in the drilled hole. But what the townspeople did not know was that two mischievous girls had gone to the drilling rig at night with a scuttleful of coal, which they dumped into the hole as a practical joke on the drilling crew. And so another dream faded.

The town was doomed to die eventually, but not until a generous portion of history had been written. But Ingalls did have a good well, located near George Ransom's saloon, and equipped with a pump and a rough watering trough hewed out of a single cottonwood log. It was a favorite meeting place for cowboys and their horses.

It so happened, not of the people's choice, that bands of outlaws found the Turkey Track and Bar X Bar ranches, with their wild and isolated hiding places, to be good hideouts. There was also a hideout on the Dunn farm. The location was a natural. The Territory's outlaws could enjoy themselves, buy provisions at Ingalls, stock up on ammunition and whisky. As time passed, these characters were welcomed more and more by the merchants of Ingalls because of the money they contributed to a poor frontier economy.

There were those in the community who knowingly sheltered the outlaws and gave them sympathy, but there were many more who did not take them in and were not in sympathy with lawlessness. Opinion was divided over just how much these men were involved in lawbreaking. They were seemingly well behaved as they moved in and out of Ingalls, quiet of manner and friendly. They played poker and drank in the saloons, furnished oysters and crackers for country dances, and took part in other community affairs. However, they refrained from taking part in any stealing or robbing in this particular community, where they wanted peace and quiet.

In territorial days, it was not wise to take sides, and a man was seldom asked where he came from or just what his business was. "The boys," as the outlaws were referred to, were seldom molested, and many of them were not suspected of being outside the law because many worked on ranches in the area between forays.

Jim Riley's ranch, where fresh horses were always available, was located on the South Canadian River near the town of Taloga, more than one hundred miles from Ingalls. It was far from any railroad and could be reached only by horseback. It was here that the Dalton gang planned their first territorial train robbery. They had been supplied with information concerning a shipment of cash for a Guthrie bank which was to arrive on the Santa Fe Railroad's Texas Express from the north on May 8, 1891. The train was scheduled to pass through Wharton (now Perry), Oklahoma Territory, at 10:50 P.M. The gang rode to Wharton, tied their horses out of sight at the stockyards north of the station, and proceeded to wait for the Express. Bill Powers remained as guard with the horses. While the outlaws waited, they discussed the possibilities of a big haul and then a quick skip out of the country and down to the Argentine and a new life, as they expressed it.

The train arrived on time and stopped at the tank for water. Bob Dalton and Bitter Creek Newcomb jumped from their hiding place behind the water tank, mounted the engine cab, and at gunpoint ordered the engineer to run the train down to the stock pens, the express car having been detached from the rest of the train. Charley Bryant and

Emmett Dalton remained with the train to be sure that no one got out of hand. Bob Dalton, Bitter Creek, Bill Doolin, and Dick Broadwell rode the train to the stock pens.

Now when the bandits boarded the train, the messenger was looking out the door of the express car. Seeing what was happening, he closed the door and locked it, began hiding all the valuables which were in his trust, and tried to plan his next move. While the robbers were uncoupling the engine and express car from the rest of the train and running them to the cattle pens, the messenger hid most of the valuables in safe places. He then locked the safe.

When the train stopped, Bob ordered the engineer down from the cab, leaving Broadwell to guard the fireman and brakeman and keep them in line. Bitter Creek and Bob then herded the engineer to the express car, where Doolin awaited their coming. Bob directed the engineer to have the messenger open the door. The messenger made a show of resistance, but soon decided it would be best to obey orders. Entering the car, the gang made for the safe and were handed a number of packages, some of which happened to be only bundles of newspapers. But Doolin discovered a package containing $500. Most of the money, however, was safely hidden in the stove and was overlooked in the hurried search of the car. The Santa Fe reported the total loss at $1,500, and the passengers were not molested.

The engine was taken back to the station, where Bryant and Emmett joined the others—the horses were near by and ready to go. The desperadoes put the loot in their saddle bags and rode off at a fast pace and were soon swallowed up by the warm blackness of the May night.

When word of the holdup reached Guthrie, a posse was organized to run the train robbers down, but by the time it reached Wharton, forty miles to the north, the outlaws were miles away. Nobody knew the direction they took. The posse, emptyhanded, returned to Guthrie. A couple of days later, the gang slipped into Jim Riley's hideout on the South Canadian. All were gaunt, trail worn, dusty, and weary from the long, hard ride, and their horses were fagged. They remained holed up in the sod shelter for a time, resting and charting their next move. They were too restless to remain in one place very long.

After dividing the loot, the gang finally decided to rob another train, which was to be selected at a later date. They then split up with the understanding that they were to meet at the Dunn farm. All of them except Charley Bryant returned to the Ingalls area. Charley went to his ranch job at a cow camp near Buffalo Springs, just over the Oklahoma Territory border in the Cherokee Outlet, seven miles north of Hennessey. Although he was in the habit of coming and going a good deal, nobody suspected him of any wrongdoing. After all, wanderlust was an affliction of many cowboys.

During the latter part of July, Bryant became ill at the cow camp, and his fever was so high that the cowboys took him to Hennessey for medical treatment. The doctor ordered him to bed, and he was placed in a room on the second floor of the Rock Island Hotel in Hennessey. Ed Short, deputy U.S.

marshal at Hennessey, was a small but courageous man and an experienced officer. He was commissioned under William Grimes, U.S. marshal for Oklahoma Territory. Short hailed from Indiana and had been city marshal of Woodsdale, Kansas, during the Stevens County war of 1886. At one time he had also served as a deputy sheriff and was at Caldwell during the turbulent days when that town was the terminus of the Chisholm Trail. An informer reported Bryant's presence to Short on August 8, 1891, and also told him of Bryant's part in the Wharton robbery and of the reward. The informer felt sure that Short would remember him when the reward for Bryant was collected.

Short arranged with the proprietor of the hotel to allow him to follow the waitress into Bryant's room when she took him his meals. To prevent Bryant from hearing more than one person coming up the stairs, Short pulled off his boots and trailed the waitress up in his stocking feet. When Bryant admitted the girl with the tray, Short covered him with a Winchester and ordered him to put up his hands. Bryant was quickly handcuffed, and while the cuffs were being fitted in place, he informed Short that no member of his family had ever been handcuffed before and that he would kill him for this injustice. But Short paid no attention to the threat. He loaded Bryant onto the first northbound train and headed for Wichita, Kansas, where some federal prisoners were jailed at that time.

Three suspicious-looking cowboys were seen around Hennessey, but it was Sunday and many people were in town for no special reason, so nobody paid any attention to them.

Short was warned by his informers, however, of the possibility that an attempt might be made to take his prisoner from him. He therefore arranged with Jim Collins, the train's conductor, to transport Bryant in the car where the baggage, express, and mail were carried. He believed the mail car would be a safer place than the passenger coach, where anyone could get to both him and his prisoner.

The train soon reached the section house at Waukomis, five miles north of Hennessey in the southern edge of the Cherokee Strip. Short asked the expressman to watch the prisoner while he stepped out on the platform to observe several men who were riding across the prairie at a fast clip. Horsemen riding toward a train were not unusual, for cowboys and Indians who had not seen a train for some time were thrilled at the sight of one. To them, it was like a circus for small boys. Short would have paid no attention to them had it not been for the warning he had received at Hennessey.

Just before stepping out onto the platform, Short gave the expressman a revolver. The expressman carelessly placed it in one of the pigeonholes of his desk and went on sorting the mail. With catlike steps, Bryant made his way over to the desk. He grasped the revolver with his manacled hands and ordered the expressman to the far end of the car. The handcuffs made it difficult to cock the gun, but he finally succeeded in getting the hammer back. Then, noiselessly, he made his way to the door and carefully opened it.

Short got a quick glimpse of his prisoner, gun in hand. He whirled with his rifle and fired at the same instant Bryant started firing. The two men engaged in a duel to the death there on the platform between the coaches. Short pumped his Winchester dry, and nearly every bullet entered Bryant's body. In spite of his shackled hands, Bryant also emptied the revolver he held. Several of the bullets entered Short's body, but some went wild. Some also went through the partition and into the passenger coach beyond, where John Dobson, a passenger who had taken refuge in the coach's toilet, was shot.

When the shooting broke out, conductor Collins stopped the train and rushed to the mail car. He found both men lying on the platform, but Short had a grip on Bryant and was trying to keep Bryant's body from rolling off the edge.

"Grab him, Jim, he's about to escape!" Short yelled to the conductor. "Help me hold him!" There was no need for Collins to help, for Bryant was dead and was slipping, not crawling, from the platform. Collins then helped Short into the car and onto a cot. "He got me, but I got him first," Short gasped. His last request was to see his mother, a request which was, of course, impossible to fulfill. In a few minutes, Short was dead.

Details of the killing were wired ahead and arrangements were made to remove the bodies at Caldwell, Kansas. Each man had received one fatal wound. A bullet from Bryant's revolver entered the marshal's shoulder and ranged down into vital organs. Short's Winchester bullet struck Bryant in the center of his chest, even with his heart, and severed the spinal column, killing him instantly. Both bodies were prepared for burial by the Schaefferr Undertaking Parlors in Caldwell. The marshal's body was shipped east to his mother, who later received Short's reward money for the capture of Black-Faced Charley Bryant. Relatives of Bryant claimed and buried his body.

Thus the first of many gun battles to the death had been fought in Oklahoma Territory. The first member of the Dalton gang, friend and saddle companion of Bill Doolin, had gone to join his Maker. And the first of many brave U.S. marshals who were to pay the supreme price for law and order in the Territory had gone to his reward. The score was now one to one. Who would be next?

3

TRAINS ARE GOOD BUSINESS FOR OUTLAWS

BOB DALTON AND HIS BOYS laid low for several months. Then Bob, gathering some information on future prospects—and prosperity—finally called the gang together at the Dunn farm, where they made plans to hold up a second train. This time it was to be a Missouri, Kansas and Texas (Katy) train. The place was to be Lillietta, a cattle-loading station four miles north of Wagoner. September 15, 1891, was to be the date. On that run, the express car would be carrying a large amount of cash. The boys all agreed to meet near Lillietta on the night of September 14 to complete their plans by going to the meeting place singly and in pairs in order to avoid arousing suspicion.

Orders were orders when given by the master of the desperado gang, so the boys appeared with alacrity and were all accounted for by sundown on the fourteenth. Emmett arrived first, followed shortly by Doolin and Newcomb, and then by Grat and Powers. The last two men to check in were Pierce and Broadwell. The gang prepared a meal over an open fire and, while they ate and smoked, made their final plans. Bob had verified the train and date, and he now directed his men to their assigned positions for the holdup. All were in agreement concerning the best procedure, and each understood what was expected of him and the importance of each man's doing his job well.

On the night of September 15, shortly after dark, the gang descended upon Lillietta and held up the station agent. They instructed him to set his semaphore and lights to halt the southbound passenger train that was soon to arrive. This was done. As they waited, a part of the gang ransacked the station for valuables while the rest kept the agent under guard, even though they had already taken the precaution of tying him up in a chair—and he was one among many.

The train arrived on schedule, and the engineer, observing the light, brought the train to a screeching halt. Even before the train came to a full stop, Doolin and Bob had mounted the engine cab and covered the engineer and crew with their guns. The rest of the gang went into action like clockwork, each to his assigned duty. First, they fired a volley of shots in order to intimidate and discourage the passengers and crew from even thinking about putting up resistance. When Emmett and Bill Powers arrived at the express car, they found it locked. Powers threatened to blast open the door with dynamite, emphasizing his threats with a couple of shots from his Winchester through the door of the car. The express messenger finally opened the door, but by this time Doolin and Bob had herded the engine crew down to the door of the car.

The messenger slid the door open and raised his hands above his head while Doolin covered him with a rifle. Bob vaulted into the car, and soon the messenger appeared at the door with a mail sack so heavy that he could scarcely lift it. However, Doolin ordered him to jump down and lay the sack on the platform. The messenger immediately obeyed, and the sack was later found to be half full of silver dollars.

Even though Newcomb and Broadwell were standing guard on each side of the train, a number of passengers fool-hardily stepped down from the cars to see what the disturbance was all about. The crowd of passengers on the platform created a threat to the robbers. To break up the situation, Bob yelled at them to get back inside the cars, which did not discourage all of them. One man had the poor judgment to pull out a small pistol. Bill Doolin ripped out a curse and yelled, "Let me at them!"

"You stay where you are ordered!" Bob shouted back, and a little later added: "We want to make a clean getaway."

Doolin ignored Bob's orders and charged down the platform, shooting into the air and yelling as he went. The man dropped the revolver, scrambled up the steps, and disappeared into the car. No attempt was made to rob the passengers, who by now had hurriedly retreated back into the cars.

Newcomb, Pierce, and Broadwell joined Emmett, Powers, and Bob at the express car door. Bob hustled the engine crew back to their jobs with orders to get under way. By this time, Doolin had rejoined the rest of the gang and was assigned custody of the mail sack, which was placed on his saddle for the getaway. It finally became so heavy that he was forced to transfer it to Bob's horse, since his own horse was growing weary under the double load of loot and man.

After riding a few hours in the direction of Ingalls, the

gang stopped to divide the loot. There was $3,000 in silver in the mail sack, which weighed 125 pounds. Emmett reported that the haul netted $19,000. It must be kept in mind, however, that outlaws liked to report large hauls, while the railroads, on the other hand, liked to play the loss down to discourage further attempts at robbery and to reassure their customers. On a few occasions, however, they seemed inclined to agree with the outlaws' report—if the shipments were heavily insured. Emmett reported the take at Wharton on May 9, 1891, at $14,000, while the Santa Fe reported a loss of only $1,500. The true picture was probably somewhere in between.

On the return trip to Ingalls and their old haunts, Doolin and three other members of the gang (probably Newcomb, Pierce, and Broadwell) met E. Bee Guthrey, editor of the *Oklahoma Hawk*, a newspaper published in Stillwater, Oklahoma Territory. Guthrey was about three miles east of Ingalls, riding horseback, on his way to the Pawnee Indian Agency when he met Doolin and the others. He noted that they were all heavily armed, with Winchesters on each saddle and heavy revolvers holstered in easy reach on ammunition belts which were well filled. Each man had a pair of shot sacks, filled with something, swinging from the pommel of his saddle. They appeared to be very heavy.

The men stopped and inquired of Guthrey whether he had seen any deputy marshals in Ingalls as he rode through. He told them he hadn't noticed any. They had started to ride on when he said to Doolin, "What have you boys got in those shot sacks?" Bill let out an oath and informed him it was none of his damned business, whereupon Guthrey very promptly agreed that it certainly was none of his business. Just as Guthrey was about to ride on, Doolin turned in his saddle, looked over his shoulder, and said, "Say, Bee, are you still running that one-horse newspaper over at Stillwater?" Bee told him yes, and Doolin asked what the subscription price was. Informed that the price was one dollar a year, Doolin reached down into one of the shot sacks, picked out a handful of its contents, and threw it, overhanded, toward Bee.

The shining objects fell to the feet of Bee's horse, and Doolin sat and watched him dismount and pick them up. After Bee had finished gathering the loot from the dust of the road, he found he was the possessor of eleven silver dollars. He told Doolin that would pay for eleven years and asked him where he should send the paper. Bill laughed and said he hadn't thought of that, but finally directed that it be sent to Ingalls until he was dead and thereafter to hell. Some years later when Guthrey sold his newspaper, he called Doolin's subscription to the attention of his successor, but he never learned whether or not the address was changed when Bill cashed in his chips.

The gang's next raid was to bring the Daltons, as well as its individual members, to greater notoriety than ever before. On the night of June 1, 1892, Bob, Grat, Emmett, Broadwell, Newcomb, Pierce, Doolin, and Powers made their way to the Santa Fe's Red Rock Station, located on the Oto Indian Reservation forty miles south of Arkansas City near the 101 Ranch. The town consisted of the depot, a section house, cattle loading pens, a store, and a few sprawling dwellings.

Its residents slumbered as the Daltons rode to the depot and took their appointed places in the darkness, waiting for the train.

The train rolled in on time and came to a stop near the depot, but no passengers got off or on. The station agent appeared to be nervous as he went to the express car and engaged the messenger in conversation. Something did not seem quite right about the train to the outlaws, so they held off action to look over the situation. The passenger coaches, their lights dimmed for the night, looked innocent enough, and the passengers, with their heads resting against the tops of the reclining chairs, also seemed to be normal enough. The first coach behind the express car was completely dark, and it seemed a little strange that all the men on the train had forsaken the smoker for sleep. Could this be a trap? Was the darkened coach filled with armed marshals, waiting for the first sign of trouble to blast the highwaymen from their boots? All of these calculations were made by the gang leader in less than a minute.

"Come on," said Grat impatiently. "We're acting like a bunch of old women."

"It's a trap," muttered Bob, laying a restraining hand on Grat's arm. "It's a deadhead and as dangerous as a rattler."

While the outlaws waited, undecided, the train pulled out. As it began to move, some of the sleeping passengers suddenly came alive and peered intently from the windows as the coaches slipped past the depot into the darkness. Something expected had failed to come off.

"I think we've been outsmarted," said Powers.

"Yep," added Doolin, "standing here like a bunch of suckers while the money got away."

"Outsmarted!" Grat exploded as he watched the red light on the rear of the train vanish in the distance. All but Bob were of the opinion that the prize had slipped from their grasp as they stood spellbound by apprehension.

The apprehension was real enough, although the outlaws could not explain it. The darkened smoker had been filled with a posse of guards headed by Deputy Marshal Heck Thomas and Fred Dodge, chief of detectives for Wells Fargo and Company, armed to the teeth and waiting for a suspicious move by anyone toward the train at any one of its frequent stops. The guard had been provided for the decoy train on a tip from railroad officials that suspicious men were in the Red Rock area.

"I thought so," said Bob, facing about as a rumble grew in the north. A second section, the regular express, came tearing in with a shrill toot and screech of brakes. It nearly caught the gang in the glare of its lights before they could fade into the shadows. "This is the one we want," commented Bob. "She's all lit up and has the right look." Powers and Grat looked a bit foolish. They reflected on what might have happened if caution had been thrown to the wind.

The gang went smoothly into action. Pierce and Newcomb jumped suddenly from the tender into the engine cab and surprised an armed guard sitting on a pile of wood in the tender, eating a sandwich. The guard attempted to jump up but fell sprawling over the wood onto the floor at the very feet of Newcomb, who disarmed him. They covered Mock,

the engineer, and Frank Rogers, the fireman, with their revolvers and ordered them to march back to the express car
and open the door. Here they were joined by Doolin, Powers,
Broadwell, Emmett, Bob, and Grat.

About this time a stout little Negro porter, as black as a
bucket of coal, stepped smartly down from the platform to
assist possible passengers on or off. Doolin spotted him and
was annoyed by his appearance on the platform, but then
Doolin was easily annoyed. "You climb back into that chick-
en coop," he threatened, "unless you want to shorten your
life span as of now!"

"Yes, sir," stammered the surprised porter as he caught the
glint of Doolin's six-gun. He hastily piled back on the train
and dashed through the coaches, shouting to the startled
passengers about the robbery and advising them to hide their
valuables at once.

E. C. Whitteny, the express messenger, and John A. Riehl,
the guard, fearing a holdup, had extinguished the lights,
locked the door, and refused entry to anyone. The gang
opened fire on the express car with rifles and six-shooters,
sending bullets plowing through the wooden walls. More
than sixty shots were fired into the car, but Whitteny and
Riehl held their fort. Bob retrieved a pick from the tender,
gave it to the fireman, and ordered him to break down the
door. This placed fireman Rogers in a tough spot: engineer
Mock realized that Rogers would probably be killed, either
by his friends on the train crew or by the outlaws, so he
pleaded with the men in the car to stop shooting.

The messenger and the guard allowed Rogers to come up

to the door, in which he was finally able to chop a hole large enough for a man to crawl through. "Now crawl in there and unlock that door, and make it damn quick!" snapped Bob Dalton. After Rogers had wiggled inside, Riehl ordered him to go to the front of the car and lie down. Next, Riehl informed the outlaws that he would shoot the first man to show his head through the hole in the door. The outlaws answered with another fusillade of shots. Then Bob ordered the men in the car to lay down their guns and come out. He promised that no one would be hurt. After a hurried counsel in the car, the three men came out and gave up.

Doolin and Grat entered the car and, with a chisel and sledgehammer, broke into the two safes and put their contents into a grain sack. They gathered up the rifles and revolvers and Riehl's gold watch, then walked to their horses and dashed off into the night. Nobody on the train offered any resistance. It was reported that the robbers had made off with $70,000—Indian money in transit to the Sac and Fox Agency. This cash, however, was on the first train, guarded by the posse, so it was safe from the robbers. The gang leader later reported they got away with $11,000, but it was more likely to have been about $3,000. The Daltons had made good their robbery threat, and without a scratch to any member of the bandit crew.

Word of the daring holdup at Red Rock was flashed over the wires to all points in the Territory. A 25-man posse under Chief Deputy Marshal Chris Madsen and the sheriff of Logan County, John Hixon, set out north and searched the Outlet for approximately sixty miles west of Red Rock. A second posse hurried south from Caldwell, Kansas. And a third posse, under the personal direction of U.S. Marshal William Grimes, raced west to the South Canadian River, while still another posse headed east from Fort Supply. Deputy Marshall Thomas and Chief of Detectives Dodge searched the Creek Nation border from the Sac and Fox Agency to the Cimarron.

The gang set a hard pace west after the robbery and rode through or along with every horse or cattle herd they came upon in order to hide their trail. They finally split up into pairs, each pair taking a different route. They all met the next morning at Jim Riley's ranch on the South Canadian and divided up the spoils. There the gang changed to fresh horses and drifted out after the split, with the exception of Doolin and Powers, who decided to stick around the ranch a while. They rode about three miles up a creek on the ranch and made camp.

The posses had searched the Territory from the Panhandle and No Man's Land to the Creek Nation, and from the Kansas border to the Canadian River. Chris Madsen and five posse members figured the gang might make for the Riley ranch to get fresh mounts and supplies. They had picked up a fresh trail in the Cimarron Hills, and it led straight to the ranch. They missed the gang by an unforgivably short time.

Powers' horse broke loose during the night and headed back to the ranch. Madsen caught the horse as it passed near where the posse spent the night. Chris carefully noted the direction from which it had come and immediately saddled up to beat the brush in that direction. After several hours of futile search, the posse gave up and headed for Guthrie, unaware they had spent several minutes under the guns of two expert riflemen who would have opened fire at any moment had they been discovered—and they didn't shoot to miss.

It was not long after the Red Rock robbery that the Daltons assembled at the Dunn farm near Ingalls to plan their next move, a more profitable job. Bob had news about a shipment of money over the Katy Railroad. Adair, a pleasant little farm town of about eight hundred people in eastern Oklahoma, not far from where the Ozarks taper off into the Neosho River bottoms, was selected. The Katy ran through the town on the Denison, Texas–Kansas City run. Unknown to the Daltons, there went out from the Dunn farm to Marshal Madsen a tip on the gang's intent to hold up the Katy in Mayes County, either at Pryor Creek or Adair—the place had not been fixed at the time. Chris notified J. J. Kinnet, chief of the Katy's detectives, of what he had learned about the Daltons' plans. He felt sure, he said, that the information was absolutely correct.

The gang arrived at Adair at 9:00 P.M., held up the agent, and ransacked the station for money and valuables. Having accomplished this, and after carefully tying up the agent, the bandits sat down in the station and coolly awaited the arrival of the northbound passenger train, No. 2. When the train pulled into Adair at 9:42 the night of July 14, 1892, the Dalton boys were still waiting. Unknown to them, however, Kinnet had thirteen guards on the train to resist any holdup attempt. The reception party was made up of Marshal Sid Johnson from Muskogee, Chief of Indian Police, Charley LeFlore, and Kinnet, all of whom were tried and proved officers who could be depended upon, but the other guards were hired pickups. These men were more boisterous and eager for a fight with the outlaws before they reached Adair than they were when the train stopped.

With the precision of experience, the outlaws went into action. Emmett and Grat swung aboard the engine cab and covered the crew. Powers, Broadwell, and Bob moved to the door of the express car from where they stood waiting on the platform. The express messenger knew what to expect and had closed and bolted the doors before reaching the station. Farther down the platform, Doolin, Newcomb, and Pierce guarded the coaches to prevent any possible interference from the passengers or the rest of the train crew.

The porter and the conductor stepped down to the platform, to be met by Doolin, Winchester in hand, who politely invited them back into the train. He also advised them to keep quiet, promising that if they did so, they would not be hurt. The officers in the smoker were aware that something was wrong, although not a shot had been fired. Peering out the windows, they saw the outlaws standing on the platform, their rifles gleaming dully in the station's dim light.

"Well, boys, here are the Daltons. Let's go," shouted Marshal Johnson as he, LeFlore, and Kinnet grabbed their rifles and made a dash to get outside and onto the platform, where they could put up a fight. As the three officers disappeared down the aisle, panic seized the deputies. Some stood transfixed, while others discarded their weapons and hid their badges, hoping that they would be mistaken for ordinary passengers. A few of the braver ones, however, mustered their courage and followed their leaders from the coach to the smoker platform—and to battle.

Emmett and Grat had ordered the engine crew down from the cab on the opposite side of the engine from the depot. Three figures scurried across the tracks and behind the coalshed. They were mistaken by the outlaws to be frightened passengers looking for a place of safety. Actually, they were Johnson, LeFlore, and Kinnet looking for a better place from which to fight.

"We expected you fellows at Pryor Creek," remarked the engineer.

"Here we are. We don't like to disappoint you all," returned Grat.

"Expected?" exclaimed Emmett, aware at once of the implication the engineer's words carried.

At that instant, rifles flashed from behind the coalshed and bullets began to clatter and scream against the engine, striking all around the outlaws and trainmen. No one was hit in the first volley, for the officers were shooting high in order to miss the train crew. The fire was instantly returned as the outlaws pumped shot after shot into the coalshed, firing blindly because it was difficult to pinpoint the exact location of the officers.

At the very first shot from the coalshed, Doolin, who was on the opposite side of the train, dropped down on one knee so that he could have a better view under the nearest car. He limbered up his Winchester as he fired shot after shot into the dark coalshed, aiming at flashes from the officers' guns.

The engineer and firemen were ordered by the officers to lie down on the ground in order to get out of the line of fire. The two required no urging as they hugged the earth. A bullet ricocheted from an engine drive wheel with a high, shrill snarl, and a second knocked over a coal scoop in the tender. And still nobody had been hit. The shooting was hot and heavy for about twenty seconds, then firing from the coalshed stopped. All three of the officers had been hit, none fatally. The rest of the guards apparently had no further stomach for the fight. A few of the deputies had made an appearance on the depot side of the train, but after exchanging a few shots with Doolin and the rest of the gang, they soon retreated to the now darkened smoker to wait it out. They hoped again that they could pass as ordinary passengers if the outlaws boarded the train.

The engineer and firemen were ordered up from the ground and around to the other side of the train, where the entire gang of thieves gathered at the express car door. Bob, Broadwell, and Powers had already taken a pick and forced open the door. Williams, the messenger, had shown no resistance after hearing all the shooting outside, but he refused to open the large safe on the pretext that he didn't know the combination. Bob fired a shot close to his head, and Williams frantically worked the dial of the safe. He was then ordered to dump the contents of the safe into a grain

COLLEGE OF THE SEQUOIAS
LIBRARY

sack, which he did without further urging. No attempt was made to rob the passengers, but the messenger's watch and everything loose in the express car was taken.

The three bandits dropped from the car to the platform with the loot. Grat and Emmett ordered the train crew aboard and on their way. There was spasmodic firing by the townspeople, which, of course, was returned. The three wounded officers were able to get back onto the train just before it pulled out.

The outlaws quickly counted noses; all were accounted for, and none had received so much as a scratch. The townspeople were not so fortunate. Dr. W. L. Gogg, a local physician who was in a drugstore near the station with another man, a Dr. Youngblood, was hit by a stray bullet and fatally wounded. The bullet severed an artery in one of his thighs and he bled to death. Dr. Youngblood was also hit by flying lead, and it was feared for a time that he, too, would die, but he eventually recovered. The entire shooting spree had taken not over fifteen minutes at the most. News of the latest and most spectacular train holdup was soon flashing over the telegraph wires. First reports had it that the Adair robbery netted $70,000, but Emmett set the figure at $17,000, and later the amount was changed to $10,000. At any rate, the gang got something worth while, but with eight men to divide the swag, individual shares were not too large.

This was the first time the Daltons had met with anything that amounted to organized armed resistance. This, together with the knowledge that an all-out effort would be made to eradicate them, was a sobering thought as Doolin and the rest of the gang rode wildly into the Dog Creek Hills. After about an hour's hard riding, they stopped to see if they were being followed. It was soon apparent that a group of riders was coming on at a very fast pace. The gang took to the brush to sit and watch, guns ready. Bob gave the order: "I will start the shooting, if it is necessary."

Soon, six young cowboys dashed by on their way to a dance. The gang relaxed and were soon on the road again. After an all-night ride, they camped at dawn near Blue Springs, east of Grand River in the Dog Creek Hills. After breakfast the next morning, the spoils were piled on a saddle blanket, then divided. Doolin and some of the others were dissatisfied, for they thought the Daltons' larger share was unfair to the other members.

After resting two days, the gang broke up. Grat, Broadwell, and Powers headed for Vinita by way of Big Cabin. Doolin, Newcomb, and Pierce stopped off at Catoosa and bought some guns and supplies as they made their way back to the Sac and Fox hideout. Emmett and Bob headed due west into the Osage country. For fear of being ambushed at the regular fords of the Arkansas, they crossed the river where it converged with the Cimarron. A thunderstorm was raging, but they made it to the opposite side after a mighty struggle. However, they lost their favorite pack horse. The animal lost its footing and was swept away by the flood, along with all of their supplies.

Emmett and Bob slept all day, resting their horses in preparation for the push west. At dawn on the third day, they camped on the banks of the Verdigris River not far from the Old Whiskey Trail, which wound down from the Kansas line through a portion of Indian Territory to the Tulsa area. They planned to make their way into the sparsely settled Osage country by way of the Caney River ford south of Bartlesville. Once there, it would be a simple matter to throw off any pursuit. If a posse were to try to take them out or cut them off from their hideout, it would be within the next fifty miles or the next twenty-four hours. A posse would seldom remain in the field more than two or three days, so with each mile they traveled west, they felt more secure. Success was again theirs.

Political pressure was brought to bear in Washington, and the territorial government and U.S. marshals were instructed to use every means in their power to bring lawlessness to a quick end, for it posed a menace to the development of Oklahoma Territory. The failure of the armed guard to prevent the holdup at Adair was severely felt by the railroads and the express companies. Passengers, traffic, and express shipments began to fall off badly as a result of the insecurity the public felt because of the many successful outlaw raids on the trains traveling through the Territory. In an attempt to stop it, armed guards rode all trains of importance in order to protect passengers and property. The express and railroad companies placed a $5,000 reward, in addition to any existing rewards, on the head of each member of the Dalton gang for their capture and conviction. This meant an offer of $40,000 by these companies alone for the entire crew. Up to this time, it was the largest sum ever offered for the capture of any band of American outlaws.

In view of this development, the Daltons felt the gang should be streamlined for the sake of mobility. Furthermore, some of the members were dissatisfied with their share of the loot. They also felt that Bill Doolin was headstrong and unruly at times, and of late he, too, was dissatisfied with the cut the Daltons gave him. It was never believed that any member of the crew was lacking in guts to go through with any emergency that might confront him. All were proved veterans of a trade where there was no room for the weak and cowardly. The Daltons thought, however, that Newcomb and Pierce were perhaps too susceptible to believing anything they heard, thus becoming a source of danger to the others.

So the gang was tentatively pared down to Bob, Grat, and Emmett Dalton, Bill Powers, and Dick Broadwell. This left out Doolin, Pierce, and Newcomb. Bob told these three that at the time he had nothing in mind for them and said he would get in touch with them later when something came up. They rode off toward Skiatook and eventually made their way back to Ingalls.

4

BILL DOOLIN GOES OUT ON HIS OWN

BY THIS TIME the territorial press had credited Bill Doolin with gunning down at least six men. He had not knowingly killed any man up to now, nor had a duel with one. If he had killed anyone, it was during a gun battle, such as the one at Adair, where everyone was shooting and no one knew who shot whom. Chances were just as good to be shot by an officer as by an outlaw, since stray bullets were all about—like bumblebees after a plow hits their nest.

Bob Dalton called the streamlined gang together on October 1, 1892, to make plans for the last and greatest raid the Daltons ever made. He planned to rob the two banks in Coffeyville, Kansas, simultaneously. Having lived there at one time, he was familiar with the surroundings and was very sure such a robbery would be a great success. It was their plan to go to South America with the loot they would get from the banks and start life anew, as they put it. Bob, Emmett, and Grat Dalton, Bill Powers, Dick Broadwell, and Bitter Creek Newcomb met at a rendezvous north of Tulsa in the Osage Nation. After an inventory, it was found that the total assets of the gang amounted to $920.

It was relatively easy for Bob to sell the gang members on the idea of robbing two banks at the same time, thereby reaping untold wealth. He pointed out that this would be an even greater feat than had been accomplished by the James or Younger brothers. It all sounded like a Sunday School picnic the way he put it.

They all saddled up on the morning of October 4, then rode about twenty miles toward Coffeyville and stopped for the night in timber on the headwaters of Hickory Creek about twelve miles from Coffeyville. During the night, however, they decided to move closer to Coffeyville, camping in the Onion Creek bottoms. Early in the morning of Wednesday, October 5, the six members of the gang rode into Coffeyville. The plan was to arrive at 9:30 A.M. Bob, Emmett, and Newcomb were to take the First National Bank, while Grat, Powers, and Broadwell were to finish off C. M. Condon's bank.

At about 9:30, they rode into town on Eighth Street and headed east. They met Mr. and Mrs. R. H. Hollingsworth near the old cheese factory, and a hundred yards down the street they passed J. M. and J. L. Seldonridge. All four of these persons noted that there were six riders and six horses. The men were heavily armed and seemed bent upon some secret mission, these persons also noticed. A short time later, Bob ordered Newcomb to swing off to the southeast and come into town from the south; in case something went wrong, he would support the gang from a different quarter. From this point on to the banks, the party of five rode in silence.

Bob and Emmett entered the First National Bank and Grat, Broadwell, and Powers walked into the Condon bank directly across the street. Despite their disguises, the men were recognized long before they reached the town square. The townspeople began to arm themselves about the time the gang entered the banks. When the outlaws stepped outside, they were met by a fusillade of gunfire from the irate populace.

Minutes later, four citizens had been killed and two wounded. Grat and Bob Dalton and Bill Powers lay dead in the street and in the alley. Emmett Dalton was near death in the alley with a bullet in his arm, another in his hip, and a charge of buckshot in his back. Dick Broadwell managed to mount his horse and hold onto the animal for a mile out of town, where he fell off and died of wounds received in the gun battle.

Emmett survived his wounds and was sentenced to life imprisonment in the Kansas State Penitentiary. He served nearly fifteen years before being pardoned. He married and moved to California, where he lived until his death, at the age of sixty-six, on July 13, 1937. He was never again involved in crime. While in California, he worked in motion pictures and was also engaged in the real estate business.

In about eighteen months, the Dalton gang had written an indelible record on the pages of the bizarre early history of the southwestern plains of Oklahoma, New Mexico, and Kansas. They gathered in an estimated $200,000. But the money didn't last long. It was soon spent on gambling, fine clothes, guns, horses and saddles, women, and liquor. Emmett Dalton once said: "There isn't such a thing as a successful outlaw. A man is a fool to try and beat the game."

Because of some difficulty he encountered and never fully

explained, Bitter Creek Newcomb arrived on the scene in Coffeyville just as the boys were making their break for freedom. He fired a number of shots from his Winchester before he finally concluded that the cause was lost. He then lit out in the direction Broadwell had taken—back to the Territory and safety. He rode hard all day and most of the night, stopping long enough for his favorite horse, Old Ben, a sorrel with a white mane and tail, to rest and blow at intervals. The last part of the trip to Ingalls was made at a slower pace; it was night, and he felt he was not being closely followed. On the morning of October 6, Newcomb's sorrel horse was in the stable behind George Ransom's house, just about all used up, and Bitter Creek was asleep in a room. Mrs. Williams, Ransom's stepdaughter, saw the horse and talked to Bitter Creek, who told her he was at Coffeyville and was damned lucky to get out alive, since the rest of the boys were all captured or killed, with the exception of Broadwell, who possibly had escaped.

While the Coffeyville raid was in progress, Bill Doolin, Bill Dalton, and Charlie Pierce were working and hiding out at Dave Fitzgerald's horse ranch eleven miles northeast of Guthrie in Cowboy Flats. Through Fitzgerald's door at one time or another passed most of the notorious territorial outlaws, of whom the Dalton gang was only one band.

At one time, Bill Doolin and George Newcomb had homesteaded in Cowboy Flats, which for a number of years after the opening of Oklahoma Territory for settlement was a rendezvous for outlaws. Fitzgerald's was one such place. Upon receiving news of the disaster at Coffeyville, Doolin began to put together his own gang, a plan he had been working on ever since he severed his relationship with the Daltons. The first man to join the Doolin gang was Bitter Creek, Doolin's old saddle pal. Next was Charlie Pierce, followed by Bill Dalton and Ol Yantis. After the Cimarron robbery came Dynamite Dick, Little Dick West, Little Bill Raidler, Bill and Bee Dunn, Alf Sohn, Bob Grounds, Zip Wyatt, and Ben Howell.

Bill Dalton had never been an active member of his brother's gang, but he had served as a spy. He located loot and learned when money would be shipped on the railroads. The law was not looking for him at the time he joined Doolin's gang.

Bill was blue eyed, five feet, eight and one-half inches tall, and had dark hair and a moustache. He was tactful, cautious, glib of tongue, and was regarded by lawmen as reckless and dangerous. Born in 1868, Bill was reported to have been a member of the California Legislature at one time. He married while in California, leaving his wife and child at her home there when he came back to Oklahoma Territory. Bill felt he should be the leader of the new gang because he considered himself the logical heir of his brother, but he had to bow to the wishes of the more experienced and expert outlaw, Bill Doolin.

Oliver (OL) Yantis was a tall, sallow-complexioned Kentuckian with overshot upper teeth. He farmed cotton on his sister's place three miles southeast of Orlando, Oklahoma Territory, when he was not engaged in outlaw pursuits with

Doolin. It was reported that on occasion he and his sister had harbored the Dalton gang, which was probably how he first met Doolin.

George Weightman, "Red Buck," was a notorious horse thief and regarded by many of the marshals as the most dangerous and inhuman of the whole lot. He was well known as a killer, for he had disposed of four men, and it was reliably reported that all that was necessary to get a man killed was to point out the victim to Red Buck and give him $50 and the job was as good as done. With him, it was simply a matter of "bushwhacking your man and forgetting the whole matter." He was a powerful, heavy-set man about five feet, ten inches tall and weighing about 180 pounds. He always wore a full moustache and his hair was a deep red, from which fact he derived his nickname.

Weightman had been arrested by Deputy Marshal Heck Thomas in 1890 for stealing some mules from Bob Knight (a horse also was stolen by him from Mun Blythe in the Cherokee Nation). He was convicted and sentenced to nine years in the penitentiary in Detroit. Weightman, along with forty-two other prisoners and sixteen guards, was put on a special train to be transported to the federal penitentiary in Detroit. En route, with a homemade saw, he and the two men with whom he was shackled managed to break loose. As the train departed from Lebanon, Missouri, Weightman and his two companions jumped out of the window feet first. The guards fired, but he was not hit. He saw his two companions fall, but did not stay to see if they were dead. He caught a freight train to Kansas and finally made his way back into the Cherokee Nation, where he hid out for the next two years.

Red Buck heard that Bill Doolin was putting together a new gang and since pickings were slim for him just then, he decided to join. Early one morning he rode into Doolin's camp with seven fine saddle horses he had stolen and which Doolin needed. He was soon one of the gang. Red Buck was never popular with the rest of the gang, however, and was regarded as a chain-harness horse thief by them.

Roy Daugherty, "Arkansas Tom," alias Bob Jones, was tall and thin with dark hair and a moustache, a straight nose, high forehead, and close-set dark-brown eyes. He was the dandy of the desperados and always appeared well dressed. He was born in Missouri, but told people he was from Arkansas. Before long, everyone was calling him "Arkansas Tom." He came from a very religious family: two of his brothers were ministers. His family had urged him to take more interest in religion, but he was not so inclined. His mother died when he was ten, and he did not get on well with his stepmother, so at the age of fourteen he ran away to become a cowboy. He went to the Cheyenne country in western Oklahoma Territory, then to Texas, where he became an expert shot and horseman. He worked for a Texas cattleman named Bob Jones for a while, and at times he passed as Bob Jones when the need arose. He later worked for a spell at Jim Riley's ranch, where he first met Doolin. He was looked upon as a gunfighter, tried and true.

Dan Clifton, "Dynamite Dick," was another cowboy and

horse and cattle thief from Texas. He spent a great deal of time around Pauls Valley, Ardmore, and the Texas line, peddling whisky as a sideline. Little else is known of his past, but he was regarded by Doolin as a good man.

Richard (Dick) West, "Little Dick," alias Dick Weston, was born in Texas in 1865. In 1881, he was employed as a dishwasher in a Decatur, Texas, restaurant, where the foreman of the Three Circle Ranch found him. In the fall of that year, the rancher took Little Dick to the home ranch in Clay County, where he worked until spring. It was there that Oscar Halsell, a Texas cattleman, became acquainted with West and hired him to ride herd on his remuda. Halsell planned a drive north with a herd of cattle purchased to stock the new ranch he was establishing, the HH, in Oklahoma Territory. Concerning West, it should be said that he was small in stature for a boy at sixteen when he joined the Three Circle outfit, but he was quick with his answers and in a short time all the cowboys had dubbed him "Little Dick." He never became larger in size, and the nickname stuck with him throughout his life.

Little Dick worked for Halsell until the ranch was abandoned by an order of the federal government so the land could be opened for settlement in 1889. Little Dick was considered a good hand, very reliable, and was entrusted with money and important missions. And it was while he worked for Halsell that he first met Doolin, who also worked off and on at the ranch between 1882 and 1889.

After the ranch was broken up, West finally drifted over into the Indian country and worked on ranches until 1892, when he joined the Doolin gang and subsequently became one of the most notorious bandits in the Southwest. He was also one of the few western gunfighters capable of using two guns with equal accuracy, one in each hand, at the same time. He was known as a savage gunfighter and dead game. Bat Masterson once said of him: "Dick West was perhaps the worst criminal in the entire Territory, outside of Bill Doolin, and the hardest outlaw in the Territory to trap. He never slept in a house summer or winter and kept moving from one place to another."

William (Bill) Raidler, called "Little Bill" in order to distinguish him from Bill Doolin, hailed from Pennsylvania and was of Dutch ancestry. Well educated, he was reputed to have a college degree. He read everything he could find on the cattle country. He first went to Denison, Texas, to work on ranches. Then he drifted north with a cattle drive and got a job with Halsell, where he met Doolin.

Jack Blake, "Tulsa Jack," was a hijacker who headquartered in the Creek Nation and was a close friend of Charlie Pierce. He had worked on the railroad at Sterling, Rice County, Kansas, for several months in 1891. Later he worked for a rancher in the same locality by the name of H. H. Whitset, then drifted down into Oklahoma Territory, where he worked as a cowboy and robbed on the side. Blake was known as a fast man with a gun, and he loved cards.

Bee Dunn and his brothers made the run into Oklahoma Territory in 1889 from Winfield, Kansas. He located on a claim on the west side of Council Creek, a little east and south of Ingalls in Payne County. Bee was rated by Deputy

Marshal Frank Canton as one of the fastest men with a hand-gun he had ever seen in action. Dunn first operated a slaughterhouse, where he killed many stolen cattle which he and his brothers had rustled. He had a partner who operated a meat market in Pawnee, where it can be inferred that much of the butchered stuff was disposed of, but he also sold meat in Perry, Guthrie, and Ingalls and rode with Doolin on occasion.

Bill Dunn, brother of Bee, with the same background and ambitions, was a little less active with Doolin than was his brother. He was very interested in the cattle business, however, specializing in stealing beef cattle. He cooperated with his brothers in harboring outlaws.

Of Alf Sohn, little is known except that he was another cowboy of unknown origin who rode with Doolin on a few occasions but was not a regular in the real sense. Bob Grounds was another of the lesser outlaws, a cowboy who rode with Doolin occasionally. Ben Howell, a third man in the same class, was associated with Doolin for only a short time before he was kicked out of the gang because he lacked sand. He then moved over to the Bill Cook gang in the eastern part of the Territory. A fourth man who could be put in this class was Bill McElheney of the old Dalton gang. He rode with Doolin infrequently and made his headquarters in the Ingalls area, where he stole cattle as a sideline.

Nelson Ellsworth (Zip) Wyatt, alias Dick Yeager, also specialized in cattle stealing, but he added a second job: robbing post offices. He was born in Indiana in 1863, the second child of John F. and Rachael Jane Wyatt. He came to

Oklahoma Territory in 1889 with his family and they settled on Cowboy Flats east of Guthrie, where he married Ann Bailey. He was a professional horseman, an expert shot, and had little respect for the law. He dearly loved to get drunk and shoot up a town. Forced to leave the Territory after one of these shooting scrapes, he went to Kansas. There he stole some riding equipment, killed a deputy sheriff who tried to arrest him, and escaped back into the Territory. Wyatt was regarded as a man of great physical strength and raw courage. He rode with Doolin on at least one major raid.

Most of the Doolin crew were destined to die violent deaths. None was hanged, but the majority died of gunshot wounds, many of them with their boots on and smoking guns in their hands on the spot where they were gunned down. Only one or two died from natural causes, and some of these were brought on by old wounds. Doolin's gang was involved in more sensational and bloody escapades than any other outlaw band before them.

For his first job, Doolin recruited Ol Yantis, Newcomb, and Bill Dalton. He had selected the little town of Caney, Kansas, as his first target; the Missouri Pacific Railroad had a station there, and the train made a brief stop each trip. The night of Wednesday, October 14, 1892, was a dark and rainy one, well suited to dark deeds. Doolin supplied his men and himself with masks to be worn during the proposed holdup, since they were becoming so well known that it was quite possible someone might recognize them. First they went to the station, where all except Yantis dismounted. Doolin directed him to the cemetery road east of town to wait with the horses.

When the eastbound passenger train, No. 182, was ready to pull out at 10:15, Doolin, Newcomb, and Dalton stepped from the shadows at the end of the station and boarded the front of the combination baggage and express car. Doolin and Newcomb climbed over the engine tender and covered the engineer and his fireman with their Winchesters. They ordered the trainmen to pull out slowly to the switch, where Bill Dalton uncoupled the express car from the rest of the train. This was all accomplished so quietly that no one in the rest of the train was disturbed. The engineer was given the go-ahead order with the express car. He could do little else with two ugly rifles staring him in the face. The train proceeded east to the cemetery, where it was ordered stopped.

The express messenger on duty was J. N. Maxwell, who witnessed the uncoupling of the express car and extinguished his lights. He barred and barricaded the doors and made ready to resist any attempt to gain entrance to his car. Doolin ordered the express car opened, but there was no reply from the now dark interior. The bandits began firing into the sides of the wooden car with their Winchesters. Maxwell fired a few shots in the dark, but without results. He finally took a bullet in the arm and decided to open the door. He was ordered by the bandits to light his lamp and toss his revolver out through the open car door. Doolin and Bill Dalton entered the car while Yantis stood guard on the ground outside. Newcomb still guarded the engineer and his crew. Maxwell was told to open the safe and hand over his personal property, including his watch. Doolin and Dalton then backed from the car and were swallowed up by the darkness. Newcomb joined the others, and they mounted and sped away to their Oklahoma hideout. Doolin's first adventure on his own was to be considered a real success, and he was already planning a bigger and better robbery for the near future.

The next trip, however, was not to rob a train. To Doolin, it seemed time to try a bank job, for there was usually more money on hand at all times at a bank, and it was difficult to get tips on rail shipments of money. It was quite possible that one might find nothing worth taking if trains were chosen at random. The members of the gang selected for this campaign were Bitter Creek, Yantis, and Doolin as commander-in-chief. The destination was to be the Ford County Bank of Spearville, a little country town of two hundred population in Ford County, Kansas, seventeen miles west of Dodge City, where it was felt that money was to be had for the taking.

In mid-October, the three desperados departed for western Kansas and Garden City, the former home of Newton Earp, half-brother of Wyatt. They arrived during the third week of October and put up at Mrs. A. C. Bacon's Ohio House. While in Garden City, they were very particular about the care of their horses and left definite instructions with John Cochran, the liveryman, concerning their feed and care. On October 28, the trio checked out of the Ohio House, secured their horses from the livery barn, and rode east.

Their next stop was at the ranch of Jonathan Lee in northern Gray County, where they spent the next day or so.

About 2:00 P.M. on the afternoon of November 1, 1892, the three entered Spearville, well mounted on their fast-running stock. They rode up to the bank, and all dismounted. Yantis leisurely led the three horses while Doolin and Newcomb walked briskly along the street toward the bank. Yantis remounted when he reached the rear of the bank. The other two entered the front door.

Doolin went to the cashier's desk and began negotiations for a loan with cashier J. R. Baird. Bitter Creek took a station at the other opening at the counter and suddenly drew his gun on the banker, exclaiming, "Throw up your hands. Throw them up damn quick, too!" Doolin drew his gun and covered Mr. Baird.

Quick as a flash, the banker dropped behind his desk, where he kept a gun for just such an emergency. Doolin immediately grasped the top of the railing and with one leap swung himself over the counter and onto Mr. Baird before Baird could get his gun into action. Newcomb also climbed on top of the railing. They held the cashier at their mercy and quickly made him turn over all the funds in sight, which amounted to $1,697 in U.S. Treasury and First National Bank of Dodge City notes. Baird was able to cover up quite a sum of gold and silver under some loose papers on his desk. This was overlooked by the bandits.

Doolin and Bitter Creek, using the cashier as a shield, stepped from the bank and raced to where Yantis waited with the horses, about fifty yards away. Baird was left behind on the street as the three outlaws mounted their horses. By the time the job was completed, Yantis had held up a man in the street who was approaching the bank. Several citizens who had just returned from a hunting trip and observed the holdup rushed to their wagons, hurriedly armed themselves, and opened fire on Yantis.

Harry Leidigh was the first to fire—with a Winchester. The outlaws returned the courtesy, firing some twenty shots as they rode out of town and headed south, pursued by as many citizens as could procure horses. At one time, J. M. Leidigh succeeded in getting close enough to exchange shots, but without effect. The citizens' horses were no match for the outlaws' superb horse flesh, and the trio soon disappeared into the brakes of the Arkansas River bottoms.

The three outlaws headed for Oklahoma Territory and their hideout. Just before dark, they stopped to rest their horses and divide the loot. When they had done this, they separated in order to throw off any possible pursuit, heading south and east, and agreed to meet later in the Creek Nation.

The gang's success could undoubtedly be credited to the generalship of Bill Doolin. He had behind him the experience of the Daltons, plus his natural leadership ability. The Doolin gang grew and prospered, following a systematic, well-rehearsed plan that included cattle rustling, horse stealing, stagecoach holdups, and train and bank robberies. Their stock in trade was dexterity with guns, excellent horsemanship, and a thorough knowledge of the Oklahoma country. Doolin's boys had one thing in common with most of the sons of the Old West: they grew up with guns and horses and learned to use both well. Doolin was a very deadly shot, but not super-fast on the draw.

The bank immediately offered a reward, and County Sheriff Charley M. Beeson sent out the following message on postcards, which he mailed all over the area:

BANK ROBBED $450 REWARD. Ford County Bank, Spearville, Kansas, was robbed today by three men. One small dark complexioned man twenty three years old, small very dark moustache and dark clothes [Ol Yantis] one medium height man, sandy complexioned, short beard, light hat and clothes [Bill Doolin] one dark man twenty five years old, medium weight, dark moustache [Bitter Creek Newcomb]. Three horses, bay, sorrel and dun, latter with line back, all medium size. Robbers have large number new $5 bills issued by First National Bank, Dodge City, Kansas. A reward of $450 is offered. C. M. Beeson, Sheriff, Dodge City, Kansas, November 1, 1892. N.B.—Keep watch for the new $5 bills.

Two weeks passed before a letter arrived from Stillwater, Oklahoma Territory, on November 15. City Marshal Hamilton B. Hueston informed the sheriff that three men answering the description of the bank robbers were in the vicinity. He asked Beeson to send someone down to make positive identification, and the sheriff indicated he would be happy to comply with the request. The man selected for this chore was John Curran of Garden City, who was a guest at the Ohio House while the three men were staying there. Curran arrived in Stillwater on November 25, and three days later, in the company of Hueston, he rode twenty miles west (which was two and a half miles south of Orlando, Oklahoma Territory), where Mrs. Hugh McGinn, a sister of Ol Yantis, lived. Ol was the suspected man.

The marshal and his partner stopped off at the house on some pretext, and both talked with Ol, who appeared to be very nervous and kept his hand near his gun at all times during the conversation. Curran immediately recognized him as one of the trio who had stayed at the Ohio House in October. Hueston and Curran returned to Stillwater and wrote Sheriff Beeson, confirming the identification of Ol Yantis. The description made identification of Yantis absolute.

On November 28, Beeson arrived in Stillwater and talked with Hueston, who told him that two of the outlaws, Doolin and Newcomb, had disappeared, but the third, Yantis, was still in the Orlando area. Beeson decided that he and Hueston would go to Guthrie to see William Grimes, U.S. marshal of Oklahoma Territory and a former sheriff in Nebraska. Beeson planned to get a warrant for Yantis and at the same time be sworn in as a territorial deputy marshal, which would entitle him to serve the warrant. They returned to Stillwater and enlisted the aid of Thomas J. Hueston, Hamilton's brother, and George Cox to make up a posse to capture Yantis.

On that same night, November 28, the four men rode to Orlando, arriving early in the morning at the R. L. Gray farm two and one-half miles south of Orlando. Gray's farm adjoined that of Mrs. McGinn. Here they left their horses and went on foot to the McGinn farm. They arrived before dawn in a heavy fog and hid themselves at a vantage point between the farmhouse and the barn and corral, hoping that Yantis would come out of the house, for they didn't want him to hole up inside.

This water color of Bill Doolin was used to publicize a motion picture entitled *The Passing of the Oklahoma Outlaws*.

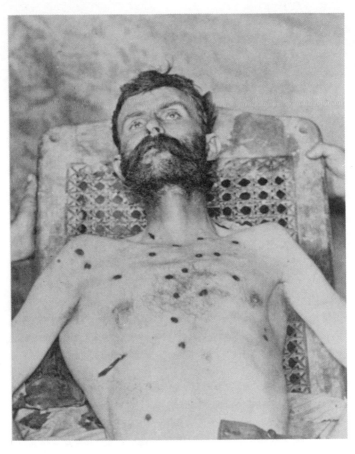

Bill Doolin as he appeared on Neal Higgins' slab. Note the twenty buckshot wounds made by the Dunns' shotguns and the one made by Heck Thomas' rifle bullet.

Edith Ellsworth Doolin, wife of Bill and
mother of Jay, as she looked in 1896.

Jay D. Meek, son and only child of Bill and Edith Doolin, at the age of sixty-six.

Courtesy Continental Oil Company

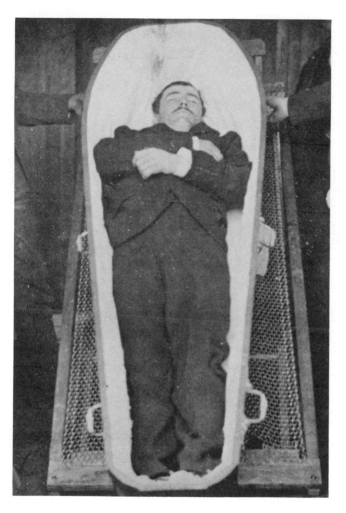

Ollie Yantis in his casket, ready for burial at Orlando, Oklahoma Territory.

Courtesy Kansas State Historical Society

Rolla Goodnight (left) and Pistol Pete Eaton were both friends of Bill Doolin and were associated with him in his cowboy days.

C. M. Beeson, sheriff of Ford County, Kansas, was chiefly responsible for the capture and death of Ollie Yantis after the Doolin gang robbed the bank at Spearville.

Courtesy Kansas State Historical Society

Eugene Manlove Rhodes, noted cowboy and author whose life was saved by Bill Doolin, about the time Doolin hid out on his New Mexico ranch in 1895.

Courtesy Alan Rhodes

A little after daybreak, Yantis came out of the back door and headed for the barn to feed his horse. He peered through the dense fog for a few minutes to see if all was well. Finally satisfied, he started walking toward the barn. When he was within fifty feet of the hidden officers, H. B. Hueston leaned toward Beeson and whispered: "That's our man. That's Ol Yantis."

The sheriff stood up and yelled at Yantis to surrender. With lightning speed, Yantis drew his revolver from a shoulder holster and fired at the sheriff. He missed. At this moment, H. B. Hueston pulled the trigger of his shotgun, leveled at Yantis, but the gun misfired. Yantis, hearing the click of the falling hammer, whirled and fired at the sound, missing a second time. Then George Cox, Thomas Hueston, and Beeson all fired simultaneously, the explosion sounding like a single report. Yantis fell backward. Beeson yelled to his men not to shoot again because their man was done for. But Yantis was far from dead. He no sooner hit the ground than he fired again, this time grazing George Cox, who swore to finish him off then and there. Beeson again interfered, stating that the man was so severely wounded that he couldn't escape.

Yantis' gun was now empty. However, he reloaded as he lay on the ground and began firing again. The possemen were unable to locate his exact position because of the gunsmoke, fog, and the lingering morning darkness. Yantis continued to fire at random until his gun was again empty. His position was revealed only by the muzzle flash. Ol's sister, hearing the shooting, ran out of the house, begging the officers not to kill her brother. Beeson told her he had no intention of killing him if he would give up his gun and surrender. She went over to Yantis, took his gun, and gave it to Beeson.

Yantis was mortally wounded and bleeding profusely. One bullet had entered his right side above his hip and ranged downward, severing his spinal column. A second bullet hit his heavy leather wallet, which contained money taken from the bank at Spearville. The wallet and bills saved him from a second severe wound, but a number of the bills were torn and pierced by the spent bullet.

Yantis was bandaged, loaded into a wagon, and hauled to the doctor in Orlando. He was put in a room at the hotel. The doctor's efforts were unsuccessful and his patient died at one o'clock that afternoon. Yantis continued to threaten revenge and cursed the officers with his last breath. He was game to the last and made no admission or confession.

After Yantis was laid out, Sheriff Beeson had a man from Orlando photograph him in his coffin, his hands crossed on his chest, leaving no hint of his violent death. The photograph was necessary in order to prove Ol's identity and collect the reward that had been offered. The photograph and other evidence was turned over to Deputy U.S. Marshal Chris Madsen in Guthrie. The body of the desperado was claimed **for burial by his sister, Mrs. McGinn. He was buried in the Mulhall, O.T. cemetery and has a large marker on his grave.**

Beeson and his posse agreed to split the reward money: $50 to each posseman and $300 for the sheriff. The money was finally paid to the officers. The first of Doolin's men had fallen, but conquering the gang would be a hard battle and long time coming.

Some time later, Yantis' mother brought suit against the marshals and the U.S. attorney for $20,000 in damages in connection with Ol's death. The case, filed at Stillwater, was thrown out of court before it came up for trial because of a flaw in the petition. The case was refiled, but before it came to trial, the courthouse burned down and all of the pertinent papers were destroyed. The suit was filed a third time, but the case was dismissed on the motion of Roy Hoffman, assistant U.S. attorney.

In all of the crimes in which Bill Doolin had been involved up to now, no definite identification had been made of him, and no warrant was specifically issued against him. Aware of this, he came and went freely in Guthrie, Stillwater, and Ingalls. One day during the early summer of 1893, Doolin and Bitter Creek came in for a drink at the Turf Exchange, a saloon and gambling hall owned by Bill Tilghman and his brother Frank, located one door from the corner on the west side of South Second Street in Guthrie. Bill ran the saloon in the front, and Frank, who was a crap-table expert, ran the gambling layout in the rear. Doolin and Bitter Creek were known in Guthrie as cowboys, and Bill Tilghman had known Doolin when he worked for Oscar Halsell.

Doolin approached Bill and said, "Mr. Tilghman, we're in kind of hard luck. Couldn't you set us up?"

"Why, sure," answered Tilghman and told the bartender, "Give them what they want."

The drinks were set out and Tilghman started to pay when Doolin said, "Wait, we can pay for them ourselves. We were just fooling."

He drew from his pocket a large roll of bills and paid with a flourish. The money was a part of the loot taken from the bank at Spearville. After separating from Ollie Yantis with their share of the money, Doolin and Bitter Creek had returned to Ingalls to lay low for a spell and plan their next move.

5

ALL THIS AND MARRIAGE, TOO

IT WAS NOT BY ACCIDENT that Bill Doolin returned to Ingalls. He had met and fallen in love with Edith Ellsworth, daughter of the Methodist preacher, notary public, and former postmaster of Ingalls. During the winter of 1891–92, she clerked in Dr. McCurty's drugstore. She also worked for Dr. Selph, as a nurse in his office, and later for Mrs. Pierce at the O.K. Hotel. Now this hotel was not a whorehouse, as it has been pictured by many, for Mr. and Mrs. Pierce reared a respectable family there and no loose woman was ever about the place. At one time, however, there was a woman of questionable character living next door.

Edith was tall and dark, with thin, prominent teeth, dark hair, and a wholesome complexion, but she was very plain in appearance. She was five feet, six inches tall and weighed slightly over one hundred pounds. She had dark, penetrating eyes and moved with a decisive step—with the air of one who knew what she was about. Her father lived on a school lease one and a half miles north of Ingalls when Doolin first began calling on Edith. At that time in 1893, Edith was working at the hotel, and her father had a general store and post office in Lawson. She was born March 15, 1873, at Marshalltown, Iowa, and was one of thirteen children. Four died in infancy, but six daughters and three sons survived to adulthood.

Doolin persistently courted Edith for several months before they decided to get married. On March 14, 1893, they caught the mail hack out of Ingalls for a point north where they were able to meet and board the Rock Island train for Kingfisher, county seat of Kingfisher County. Here, the next day, her twentieth birthday, Edith became Mrs. William Doolin, wife of the most notorious outlaw in the Southwest, a man with a bounty on his head. It is quite fitting and only fair to state that Edith Doolin was loyal to her husband, even to the bitter end—and a bitter end it was to be.

The couple soon returned to Ingalls, where Edith worked for Mrs. Selph, as well as in the doctor's office. The Doolins established a home between Wagoner's blacksmith shop and the hotel (Mrs. Pierce was her closest friend). She was regarded in the community as very efficient in handling the sick. Here Bill would visit her when possible. So wary was the couple, and so strange their actions at times, that it was quite some time before anyone learned Doolin was married, and it took even longer to find out to whom he was married.

At about the time of Doolin's marriage to Edith, Bitter Creek became interested in a waitress at the Nix Restaurant: Sadie Conley (nee Sadie McCloskey), widow of Deputy U.S. Marshal John Conley, who was killed during a gun battle in a saloon at Cushing (Old Town) by the saloon's owner, a man named Johnson. Sadie lived with Edith when Doolin was away. As time passed, people began to say that

Bitter Creek and Sadie "kind of lived together." As far as is known, they were never married.

It has never been established whether or not Edith knew Bill to be an outlaw before they were married. He had courted her in a grand manner, taking her to dances and to all the country socials. She knew him as a cowboy when they first met, but may have guessed the truth about him before they were married. When he asked for her hand, she could but say yes.

After their marriage, she realized her husband was one of the most desperate outlaws of the Southwest; he was being hunted all over the Territory and was unable to come home for months on end. He was forced to elude lawmen by long, hard rides at night and spend a few fleeting hours at her side. But she stood by him in all of his lawless deeds until finally, on an August night, she sobbed in grief as she saw his bullet-riddled body stretched prone on a dusty, lonely Payne County road.

Once safely back in Ingalls, Doolin was planning another and greater adventure in crime. This time he selected the Santa Fe Railroad's California Express for his target at a spot one-half mile west of Cimarron, Kansas. Doolin carefully calculated that he would need five men for the job, including himself. After considering the qualifications of each, and remembering the weakness found in Ollie Yantis, he selected Bill Dalton, Arkansas Tom, Bitter Creek Newcomb and Tulsa Jack Blake for his raiding crew.

Doolin and his men selected the fastest of their riding stock and headed for Kansas. They spent the night north and west of the Cimarron River and stopped off at a ranch four miles north of the Cimarron for dinner and supper. They rested their horses and gave them a good feed on grain purchased from the rancher. At sundown, they all rode south to a point one-half mile west of the town of Cimarron near a bridge on the Santa Fe's transcontinental line to California.

As the westbound California Express neared the spot at 1:20 A.M. on the morning of June 10, 1893, Tulsa Jack flagged it down. Before the train could come to a full stop, Bill Doolin and Bill Dalton swung onto the locomotive from opposite sides and covered the engineer and fireman with their heavy revolvers. All of the outlaws were masked. Doolin ordered the engineer to pick up a sledge hammer and go to the express car. Tulsa Jack, Arkansas Tom, and Bitter Creek joined the other two as they marched the two trainmen before them. Doolin ordered the express messenger, E. C. Whittlesey of Kansas City, to open up. He refused and the outlaws fired a number of shots into the car, but the messenger still failed to obey their orders. The engineer was then ordered to break open the door with the hammer. When the door was finally broken open, they saw that the messenger had been wounded in the left side and disabled.

Doolin and Dalton entered the car, and Whittlesey was ordered to open the through safe. He could not, so the outlaws had to be satisfied with the contents of the way safe, which were hastily stuffed into a sack. Part of the money, $1,000, was in silver deposits for the bank at Trinidad, Colorado. Meanwhile, the other three outlaws remained outside and fired at the passenger cars, shouting orders to intimidate the travelers.

The express messenger had been able to hide $10,000 in currency and some jewels, which were not found by the outlaws. Doolin set up a cot for the wounded messenger and put him on it before leaving. No attempt was made to rob any of the passengers, and as soon as the express car was cleaned out, the gang fired a parting shot, mounted their waiting horses and put the spurs to them, and dashed off to the southwest toward Oklahoma Territory.

The train was quickly run back to the station at Cimarron and the alarm given. The sheriff wired the marshal's office in Guthrie, where Chris Madsen was on duty. He was informed that the five outlaws would probably cross the Cimarron River at Deep Hole, not far from Ashland, Kansas, and would undoubtedly enter the Territory about where the town of Buffalo, in Harper County, Oklahoma, is now located.

Chris immediately wired the commanding officer at Fort Supply, Oklahoma Territory, to get a posse of Indian scouts together and send them to Woodward Station, where he would meet them and direct the posse in person. The sheriff at Cimarron formed a posse and took off in hot pursuit, but was able to track the outlaws only a few miles to the spot where they stopped and divided their loot. They had dropped some silver dollars, which indicated to the sheriff they had been there.

After dividing the loot, the five men rode south. However, Tulsa Jack soon left the group and rode off alone. The remaining four rode to the Del Hess ranch just east of Blue

Grass Post Office in Beaver County, where they stopped for a meal. After eating, they again took to the road.

Shortly after Doolin's departure from the Hess ranch, Frank Healy, the sheriff of Beaver County, arrived and drafted a posse to capture the outlaws. This was a good time, he thought, to collect that $5,000 reward which read "dead or alive." He put together a posse from the Blue Grass neighborhood made up of Del Hess, John Marshall, J. T. Stanley, George Petty, Tom Seward, and possibly others. They were joined by Bill Corn and George Gillion from Englewood, Kansas.

The posse spotted the outlaws a few miles south of the present site of Laverne, Oklahoma, and one man was sent to Fort Supply for help. The soldiers were asked to go to Wolf Creek and head off the fleeing outlaws, but they were too slow in getting started because of the red tape involved in sending troops on this kind of an expedition. So the outlaws were able to elude Healy and his posse, who finally abandoned the chore and went home.

Soldiers and Indian scouts were waiting for Madsen on his arrival at Woodward. The officer in charge told him the troops could not be used except on the Indian Reservation, and the Indian scouts were not too eager to engage the outlaws in battle. Nevertheless, they set off in search of Doolin and his four companions at the place where they were expected to enter Oklahoma Territory. Chris sent out half the scouts to see what they could turn up, and it was not long before they reported seeing four horsemen, well mounted, traveling south at a fast clip. Chris reasoned that this must be the Doolin gang, and he was right.

By doing some hard riding and keeping out of sight, Chris and his posse were able to get ahead of the outlaws and take them by surprise. But the latter were not so surprised that they couldn't shoot back, so the two groups exchanged a few shots.

The outlaws were not too concerned about getting away; they knew the rifles used by the Indian scouts were of ancient vintage and did little more than make a lot of noise with great puffs of smoke. It was a different matter, however, when it came to the rifle Chris used, for he had a new .30-.30 Winchester that employed a steel-jacketed bullet. It had a greater range and more accuracy than the old lead ball. Chris began firing away with his new gun, and by a stroke of luck, he shot Bill Doolin in the foot. The bullet entered Bill's right heel and followed the arch to the ball of the foot, where it shattered the bone into many small pieces, making a painful and serious wound.

As soon as Doolin was wounded, the outlaws put spur and quirt to their horses and left for parts unknown, disappearing in a large willow thicket north of the present town of Fargo, Oklahoma. They soon separated and rode in different directions in order to avoid pursuit and to confuse the Indian trackers. Arkansas Tom took Doolin to Jim Riley's ranch, where he knew outlaws were always welcome. The Indian trackers, hampered by the split-up and by oncoming darkness, finally had to give up the search when they lost the trail. Chris called off the pursuit and they returned to Fort Supply. Meanwhile, Doolin made good his escape, but the long arm of the law was coming closer.

By the time the outlaws reached Riley's ranch, Doolin's foot was so badly swollen that it was necessary to cut his boot away before the wound could be dressed. He was then put to bed. The next morning, the foot was much worse and so inflamed and swollen that it was decided to take Bill to a doctor for treatment. Arkansas Tom, with Doolin on horseback, took off for Ingalls, the closest place where a doctor who could be trusted to aid the outlaws could be found. It was a hard, rough ride, and a man of lesser nerve would not have made it.

Upon their arrival at Ingalls, Tom was informed that Dr. Selph was out of town and would not be back until the next day, so Tom and Doolin put up at the O.K. Hotel to await the doctor's return. Doolin's foot had been neglected for so long and was so painful and badly swollen by now that he could not bend down to reach it. Mrs. Pierce brought out on the hotel porch a pan of hot water and a bottle of carbolic acid, the regular home remedy at that time for infections, and began to bathe the foot. Bill McGinty, an old-time cowboy, came by about this time and offered to do the bathing. He and Doolin had punched cattle in the Territory at the same time and had known each other for years, but McGinty was unaware of how Bill had been hurt.

Heck Thomas happened to be in the Ingalls area looking for Doolin at that precise moment, and while Bill was bathing the foot, Heck came up the sidewalk. Doolin advised Mc-

Ginty to get out of the line of fire, for he fully expected Thomas to draw on him, but the marshal passed by, seemingly unaware of Doolin's presence on the front porch of the hotel. Had Thomas gone for his gun, he probably would have been a dead man because Doolin had seen him first and was armed and ready for him.

Doolin continued to suffer intense pain in his foot, and when Dr. Selph returned and examined it, he found it necessary to remove the bullet. Doolin carried it in his pocket for years. The doctor also had to remove many pieces of shattered bone, which meant that the wound was long in healing.

Doolin had a permanent limp from that time on, and the foot always gave him trouble, which became progressively worse as he grew older. Long before the wound had healed, however, Doolin decided he could tarry no longer in Ingalls, for the marshal might show up at any time and he must be on his way to a safer hiding place. When Dr. Selph had treated and bandaged the foot for the last time, Doolin asked him how much he owed him and the doctor answered, "Just whatever you think it's worth, Bill." Doolin pointed to sacks of money on a small table and told the doctor to help himself. To this offer the doctor replied: "No, I'll not do that, Bill. I don't have any price for this work. Whatever you think is right, and I'll be satisfied." Doolin reached into his money belt and handed the doctor two twenty-dollar bills.

Dr. Selph treated Doolin's men many times for sickness and injuries, mostly gunshot wounds, and such calls were generally made at night. When it became necessary to make a call on one of the wild bunch, the doctor would put out all the lights in his house to give the appearance that the family had retired for the night. Then he would silently leave to go on his call. Most of these were made on foot because the outlaws would not consent to his riding, for fear someone would see him or follow him and locate their hiding place. In such an event, the doctor might unwittingly meet a Doolin enemy in the shadows, who would in this way know that one of the desperados was sick or hurt and could be captured. Dr. Selph was not too eager to be seen either, for a raid might be conducted while he was treating an outlaw, and he had little desire to be present on such a warm occasion. At times, it was necessary for the doctor to crawl through the brush on his hands and knees in order not to be observed while making a call.

One night Dr. Selph was called out to treat Tulsa Jack Blake for a gunshot wound. Upon examination, he found that the bullet had entered and passed through the patient's thigh, entered the large muscle of the femur, from which it had come out just above the knee, then dug into the calf of the leg to exit again at the ankle. It then passed into and through Blake's heel and lodged in the sole of his foot. When asked how it happened, Tulsa Jack said that he was lying on the ground, face down, with his head uphill while taking a nap in the warm sun. To put it in his own words: "Some old nester took a shot at me with an old squirrel rifle." Blake finally recovered from the wound, but he was a sore man for quite a spell, especially in the saddle.

Doolin didn't leave the area just then, but moved out to Bee Dunn's farm for a while to let his foot heal and his absence in town to be noted. Edith visited him, and as his foot healed, Doolin spent time with her in Ingalls, where she was still working at the O.K. Hotel. He walked with a crutch, or used his Winchester as a crutch, for a long time after he was wounded. The boys joshed him about running when he was shot in the heel from the rear.

Like all the other outlaws of his day, Bill Doolin had a favorite hideout. It was in Payne County at the headwaters of Turkey Creek under a large, flat rock. There was a cave large enough to hide both the outlaws and their horses. Another hideout was south of the town of Yale among the large rocks along the riverbank. Mrs. Lizzie Lemmons took food to the outlaws here on many occasions, saying she would tell lawmen she had seen no one. She always felt that "the boys" would have been willing to quit their outlawry if they had the chance.

In the 1890s, B. F. Ramey ran a saloon and livery stable in Stillwater. Doolin would tell Ramey's stable hand to leave his horse saddled all day for a quick getaway. At about 10:00 P.M. each night, he would ride out, or if he planned to spend the night, he would ask that the horse be unsaddled. Next morning, he would have his horse saddled again and waiting. On one of his visits, Bill pulled his gun on a friend of Ramey's who had addressed Ramey affectionately as an "old S.O.B." The friend was very fond of Ramey, else he would not have said what he did. Ramey explained the situation to Bill, whereupon Bill replied that nobody could speak to a friend of his in such a manner.

The gang had many friends among the settlers. Emerson

Soric, a pioneer of Falls City, Payne County, Oklahoma Territory, related an incident that shows why:

> Sis had baked a big bakin' of lightbread and stored it in a big stone jar covered with a tight wooden cover. That afternoon we all went to town to the store, and when we got back and went to get a loaf of bread for supper that night, there wasn't any. But wrapped in brown paper in the bottom of the jar was a package. We unwrapped it and found a ten-dollar gold piece. There was a note with it that said: "Thanks for the bread. We can get money easier than bread like this."

There were other incidents in which Doolin scattered good will. The tales are many of the good deeds credited to Doolin. Warney Pickering relates that as a boy in Ingalls, he had a lemonade stand one summer and Bill Doolin bought six glasses from him just to help him out. He staked many a broken-down sodbuster and bought him a meal and grain for his horse, and perhaps he stayed the night at many an out-of-the-way homestead.

A farmer by the name of Burch lived on a homestead near Ingalls, and each year he grew a large field of watermelons. The going price was five cents a melon. Bill Doolin, without fail, paid ten cents each for the ones he bought, mentioning to Burch that if a watermelon wasn't worth ten cents, it wasn't any good, so he always paid the dime. Years later when money was being donated for the marker for Bill's grave in Summit View Cemetery at Guthrie, the son of Mr. Burch told the story as he made a contribution on the strength of Bill's generosity to his father at a time when five cents was to be appreciated but a dime was something else.

Bill Doolin and his men camped out a lot, and one night they camped by a creek. Not far from their camp were two other men camping down for the night, drifters going west. After supper, the two strangers came over to Doolin's camp. One of them had a Marlin rifle in his hands, and he saw among Doolin's weapons a ten-gauge shotgun to which he took a fancy. He asked about it and suggested a trade. A deal was finally made, and Doolin gave the man the gun for the price they agreed upon, with some boot. The stranger opened his wallet and paid the boot in cash on the spot. There was $1,300 in that wallet. The gun trader was really shook up the next day when he learned with whom he had made the shotgun trade.

Many of the older residents of Ingalls recall the night Bill Doolin was attending church in a brush arbor near the main street in the northwest part of town. The Reverend Charles C. Platt was halfway through his sermon when a disturbance outside nearly broke up the meeting. A bunch of the local boys had decided to have some fun. Bill Doolin was near the front of the congregation, his short Winchester saddle gun across his lap, and Bitter Creek stood at the rear in the shadows on guard. Bill got up and, holding his rifle close to his legs as was his custom, stalked down the center aisle and outside.

Doolin informed the boys if they didn't shut up, he planned to ventilate some of them with hot lead. From then on, the service was as quiet and orderly as a Puritan Sunday School. There have been few times, even in the Old West, when reverence has been preserved in religious services at the point of an outlaw's rifle.

Bob Beal ran a general store in Ingalls for a number of years. One day Bill Doolin sat propped up against the wall in a cane-bottomed chair on the porch near the door of Beal's store with a Winchester across his lap. A down-and-out sodbuster drove a lanky team hitched to a farm wagon up to the hitching rail and tied them up, although in their emaciated condition it hardly seemed necessary. He stepped down from the wagon, spoke to Bill, and passed into the store. Bill could hear the conversation within the store from where he sat. The man made a plea for credit to buy some sidemeat and flour, saying his family was without supplies and hungry. Beal was very sympathetic, but explained that he had out more credit than he could afford already, so he could do nothing for the man.

The homesteader turned dejectedly around and walked out on the porch, took off his old floppy hat, and mopped his brow as he gazed into the hazy distance. Doolin slowly got up from his chair and, carefully surveying the stranger, asked: "Did I hear you say that your family is hungry?"

"Yes," answered the man, "but I don't know what I'm going to do."

"Come with me," Bill said as he turned back into the store. "Bob," he asked, "is my credit any good here?"

"Sure is," Beal replied, "Why?"

"Let this man have what he needs and if he doesn't pay for it, I will."

The man got his needed supplies, and that fall he paid up

in full. Small wonder that Bill Doolin had friends among the homesteaders!

It was a custom in that locality to have a dance at someone's home each Saturday night nearly the year round, and many of the dances were held at Ed Williams' log house a couple of miles west of Ingalls. The place later became the hiding place of Marshal Lafe Shadley's gun for a while. The Meyers boys usually fiddled and called for most of these country dances, to which everyone came from far and near. It was not uncommon for Doolin's boys to show up with oysters for stew and enough salt crackers for all. It must be kept in mind that at this time store-bought salt crackers and oysters were not only a delicacy but cost real money, of which there was not enough in the new territory. Doolin always insisted that the windows of the house in which the dance was being held be darkened because someone might take a shot, even though a guard was usually posted outside to watch for unwelcome lawmen who might happen to pass that way.

Bill Doolin always paid generously in cash for things he bought—and cash was a commodity in short supply. Cash was very welcome to one and all in the Territory, since there were always more needs than money with which to buy.

For example, local prices might run this way: coal oil (kerosene), 20¢ per gallon; seven bars of White Russian soap, 25¢; axle grease, 5¢ a box; Lion or Arbuckle coffee, 20¢ a pound; three-pound can of tomatoes, 7¢; pail of jelly, 40¢; pail of syrup, 50¢; twenty-five pounds of rice, $1; seven pounds of oat flakes, 25¢. Men's suits sold for $4.50, felt hats for $1, and ladies' hats 50¢ each. Ladies' fine hand-sewed shoes were $1.89 and pure French kid oxfords 89¢. Other items were priced accordingly.

Bill Doolin had an iron-gray horse, a particular favorite, that he called "Possum." He rode this horse on many of his "business trips" when he would need the best and speediest horse possible. Joe Simmons has often told a story about Possum. When the weather was good, it was Bill Doolin's custom to hide out in the brush and timber while he slept, especially if there were marshals prowling about. On one of these occasions, when there seemed to be a great number of lawmen in the vicinity, Simmons decided to go fishing on Council Creek. He took his pole and tomato can of red worms and started down through the timber to the creek, picking his way very carefully through the thick underbrush. Suddenly he stepped into a clearing where a man lay sleeping in the warm spring sun. A large gray horse stood grazing near by. As Joe stepped into the clearing, Possum suddenly threw up his head, gazed for a moment, then stepped briskly over to the side of the sleeping man and nudged him sharply in the ribs. At the first nudge, Bill Doolin sprang to his feet, revolver in hand, leveling it at Simmons. Joe was quick to shout, "Don't shoot, Bill! It's me, Joe Simmons!"

This same horse stood many a long night's vigil over his master while Doolin got some much needed sleep and rest after outdistancing a posse. Fate decreed that the man and his horse must part: Bill was forced to trade off Possum because everyone in the Territory got to know the horse and it became too easy to spot Bill Doolin, who was a wanted man with a price on his head. With each passing day, more and more men were trying to collect the reward.

After the Coffeyville bank robbery and the elimination of the Dalton gang, Bill Doolin and his cohorts became Oklahoma Territory's Public Enemy No. 1. It was then that the territorial marshal's office turned all its energy toward eradicating Doolin and his gang.

In early June of 1893, Bill Doolin, Bitter Creek, Arkansas Tom, Dynamite Dick, Tulsa Jack, Red Buck, and Bill Dalton began to drift into Ingalls. Within a short time, all were staying in town except Bill Dalton, who put up at Bee Dunn's farm and rode back and forth to town each day. All the men were heavily armed with Winchesters and Colts and were on guard at all times—and they generally traveled in pairs. Most of them boarded at the O.K. Hotel and played cards and did their drinking in old man Ransom's saloon. They kept their horses stabled at George Ransom's livery barn, just south of the saloon, and they all lived at Bee Dunn's when not in town.

Ransom's Saloon was of the frontier type and not very pretentious. It was housed in a small frame building with an icehouse tacked on the back, as if it were an afterthought. The south side of the barroom was provided with poker tables and chairs, and there was a small tobacco case at the east end near the door. The backbar, which provided shelf space for the liquor stock and glasses, was overhung by a large, long mirror. And hanging nearby was the usual nearly nude picture of a buxom woman in a reclining position, her long, dark hair flowing about her head and shoulders. Kerosene lamps hung from the ceiling, and there was a brass cuspidor or two along the wall. These items made up all the fixtures of the place.

Serving behind the bar, in addition to the owner, George Ransom, and his helper, Murray, was the regular bartender, Leamon Myers, who was a former cowboy on the XIT Ranch in Texas before coming to Oklahoma Territory in 1890.

Whisky sold for a dime a shot, and if you wished, you could have a large glass of cold beer for the same price. No fancy mixed drinks were served; the customers took their drinks straight, and there was a keg of ice water on the back end of the bar for anyone who needed a chaser. Free whisky for loafers out of funds was provided from a bottle, kept under the bar, with a funnel in it. Into this bottle went what the paying customers left in their glasses. When a fellow came in broke and "just had to have a free drink," on the house, this was what he got. Redtop rye whisky, the best, sold over the bar for 15¢ a drink but was sold for 50¢ a pint to go.

The outlaws were more law abiding than many of the citizens and were regarded as good for business because they nearly always had money to spend. They would drink for a while, then throw a fifty-dollar bill on the bar, or a ten, or a five, and never ask for the change. Doolin's boys seldom got drunk and were never bad to fight, and the sawed-off shotgun under the bar was never needed when they were around.

The boys got a little boisterous at times, however. It was great sport to shoot the whisky glasses off the top of the bar with their .45s, and this made it necessary to plane down the bar from time to time to remove the bullet marks. On one such occasion, Bitter Creek was happy and having a lot of fun throwing beer on the boys at the bar. While he was moving about to throw the beer, the hammer of his .45 caught in a hole inside his coat where it had worn through and the gun discharged. Bitter Creek jumped as if he had been shot and went for his gun. However, as it cleared leather, he could find no one with a smoking six-gun to shoot. The boys all had a good laugh at Bitter Creek's expense, and another round of drinks followed.

After playing cards and drinking for several hours without interference, Doolin and the others usually saddled their horses at the livery stable and rode out to Bee Dunn's farm to eat and spend the night. The next morning, Doolin and his five henchmen would return to Ingalls for another game of poker and liquid refreshments, but they never got drunk as a group.

On occasion, the Dunn boys—Bee, John, Dal, and Bill—rode with the Doolins, especially Bee. The Dunns were known to the marshals as cattle thieves who had harbored outlaws for many years at their farms and ranches in the Ingalls neighborhood.

Finally, all of Doolin's gang put up at the O.K. Hotel, that is, with the exception of Doolin and Bitter Creek, who took board and room with Mrs. Ransom, where Bill McGinty also lived. Dalton preferred to sleep out or ride the ten miles back and forth to the Dunns' rather than remain in town where the marshals might find him.

One of Marshal E. D. Nix's deputies was a large Negro named Charlie Petit. Petit was very eager to collect the reward for the capture of Bill Doolin and boasted that he would take him, so he went to Ingalls and hung around the saloons. One day he was leaning on the bar having a drink when Doolin walked up to him and said, "I hear you've got a warrant for my arrest. Now don't lie to me. If you've got it, don't tell me you haven't."

"Er, er, yessir, Mister Doolin. Uh, I've got one for you, but, uh, I wasn't goin' to serve it!"

"Let me see it," Doolin demanded. After he had read the warrant, he handed it back to the Negro and said, "Now let's see how fast you can eat it."

"Yessir, Mister Doolin," said Petit, as he stuffed the warrant into his mouth. When he had it entirely chewed, Doolin said to the bartender, "Now, give him a whisky for a chaser."

Doolin then told Petit: "Now let me tell you something. If you ever take another warrant for me, or if I ever hear of you carrying one, or if you ever show up here again, I'll kill you on sight."

"Nossir, Mister Doolin," answered the deputy. "I won't carry no more warrants for you."

"Now," said Doolin, "let's see how fast you can get out of town." At this invitation, the deputy mounted his horse and lost no time leaving Ingalls.

There was the occasion when a boy and his father, riding in a buggy, overtook Deputy Marshal John Spurgeon on horseback searching for Doolin, who was reported in the vicinity. The boy's father asked the deputy to get in the buggy and ride with them, which he did. They had not gone far, perhaps two miles, when they saw a man on horseback approaching. As he drew near, both men recognized him as Bill Doolin. He came on and they met. Not a word was spoken by anyone, and no move was made by Spurgeon, who was known to Doolin. He knew it would be suicide to make an attempt to arrest the outlaw, so he didn't try it.

6

GUNFIGHT AT INGALLS

WORD REACHED THE OFFICE of Marshal E. D. Nix in Guthrie that Doolin and his boys were making Ingalls their permanent headquarters and that they were all in the town most of the time between jobs. The marshal's forces got their heads together and began to formulate a plan whereby the gang could be captured in a group and the rewards collected. Such a plan, if successfully carried out, could rid the Territory of its greatest source of trouble. The final decision was to send two deputies, unknown to the outlaws, to Ingalls posing as surveyors. They were to circulate the story that they were making a survey for a proposed railroad to go through Ingalls. The town had been trying for a long time to get a railroad, and it was felt that the people there would welcome such a project with open arms and would not be suspicious about the presence of a "railroad surveying crew."

Deputies Red Lucas and Doc Roberts were selected. They were outfitted with a covered wagon, supplies, surveying instruments, and a good team of horses. They arrived at Ingalls and pitched camp near Ransom's Saloon late in July, 1893. They were soon going to the saloon each night after returning from the day's surveying, playing cards and drinking with the outlaws. Both men were considered by the outlaws as good fellows and were accepted at their face value.

Lucas and Roberts finally left Ingalls for a week, but returned with the story that they were back to locate a booth for interested settlers to register for certificates entitling them to race for land and town lots along the new railroad right-of-way. They also returned to their old haunts at the saloon and gambling tables, drinking and gabbing with Doolin and his pals.

One night while the poker game was going strong and Red Lucas was sitting in, a man known to them as "Ragged Bill of Stillwater" came into the saloon and wanted in the poker game. Bill Doolin, who was having a run of high good luck, gave Ragged Bill twenty dollars' worth of chips for a twenty-dollar gold piece. Within a short time Ragged Bill was broke, and since Doolin was still winning, he gave the man fifteen dollars' worth of chips and received an I.O.U. in exchange for them. Shortly thereafter, the saloon doors opened and in stepped Bob Andrews, deputy sheriff of Payne County, who was known to each of the outlaws.

The poker game stopped. Not a chip rattled nor a card fell, and not a person moved. All eyes were riveted upon the deputy sheriff, and each outlaw had his hand near his gun for a quick draw. Bob Andrews held up his gun hand in a gesture of peace and said, "Boys, I'm after that man over there," his finger pointing to Ragged Bill, whom he ordered to stand up. Bill got up and said he wanted a word with Doolin. Andrews nodded, and the two of them, Doolin and Ragged Bill, went over to a corner in the rear of the saloon. Everyone kept his place at the table, motionless but watchful. Bob Andrews knew that Red Lucas was a deputy marshal, but did not dare speak to him or give any sign he had ever seen him before.

Ragged Bill told Doolin he had knocked an old man in the head in Stillwater and robbed him of forty dollars. He had promised to give a man known as Long Tom half the money. The robbery was the reason he was being arrested by Andrews. He further said that he had come to Ingalls to join the Doolin gang and asked that they not let the deputy take him back to Stillwater to stand trial.

"Bill," Doolin said, "you're a low-down polecat to knock an old man in the head for forty dollars, and I wouldn't let you carry water for my bunch." He turned Ragged Bill over to Andrews and told the deputy to put handcuffs on him. As the two started to leave the saloon, Doolin happened to think of the fifteen dollars Bill owed him from the poker game, so he told Andrews: "Wait a minute. That son of a gun owes me fifteen dollars, and I will have to hold him until I get my money."

"O.K., Bill," said Andrews. "I'll see that you get your money." And with that promise from Deputy Andrews, Doolin let them pass out into the darkness of the night. It had been a rather strained situation in view of the fact that Doolin had a price on his head and was dealing with a man of the law. Unknown to any of the others present, however, Doolin and Andrews were reported to be related by marriage, so Doolin had little to fear. The deputy was also outnumbered seven to one, and because of their relationship, Doolin felt Andrews would keep his word.

Andrews started back to Stillwater with his prisoner im-

mediately. Along the way, he met Long Tom, who was looking for Ragged Bill in an effort to collect his half of the forty
dollars. When he saw that Bill had been captured and that
Andrews did not know of his part in the robbery, he merely
spoke and rode on over to Ingalls, where he got into the same
poker game so recently vacated by his partner. The game
lasted until very late that night and was resumed again early
the next morning. It was about 10:30 A.M. when Andrews
walked into the saloon the second time. He stated that he had
returned to arrest Tom for his part in the robbery of the old
man at Stillwater. Long Tom rose from the table and said he
would not go. He stood in the gunman's crouch, his hand
hovering over his .45.

"Stop, Tom!" Bill Doolin shouted. "You and I have rode
herd together and slept under the same blanket in times past,
but I have gone on the wrong side of the law and can't turn
back. You are just starting, so go back with Andrews, stand
trial, and go straight after you pay your debt to society. I have
been scouting on the wrong side of the law for a long time
and I know it is no good."

Although he was a notorious outlaw, Doolin had many
friends and prevented many men from going wrong. He
always advised them, when they wanted to join his gang after
some misdeed, to give up, take their medicine, and go straight.
Doolin ended life as an outlaw, but there were many who
knew him as a square shooter.

Tom told Doolin he wasn't going because they would keep
him in jail a year or more before he would be brought to trial.
Doolin asked Andrews if he would see that Tom was freed on

bond until his case came up for trial, and Andrews gave his promise that he would, even if he lost his job over it. Then Doolin said to Bitter Creek: "Get our horses out of the livery barn. I'll ride with Tom, and you ride with the sheriff behind us."

The two outlaws didn't take Andrews' gun, just trusted him not to start anything. When they reached the edge of Stillwater, Doolin said, "Andrews, I'm taking your word that you won't put Long Tom in jail, and if you doublecross me, well, we'll meet sometime." Andrews replied drily: "Doolin, you have my promise. And by the way, here is the fifteen dollars I told you I would collect from Ragged Bill." With these parting words, the four men separated, Doolin and Bitter Creek riding back to Ingalls, and Andrews, true to his word, going on to Stillwater with Long Tom to make his bond.

The first week in August, Red Lucas and Doc Roberts hitched up their team and pulled out for Guthrie to report to the marshal's office and make plans to capture Doolin and his entire gang. Dynamite Dick was the only one to suspect Lucas and Roberts, but Doolin felt that his fears and suspicions were groundless. Upon receipt of the report from the deputies, Marshal Nix immediately gathered a posse to capture or exterminate the Doolin gang. Deputy U.S. Marshal Bill Tilghman was Nix's choice to take charge of the expedition, but because Tilghman had a broken ankle, U.S. Marshal John Hixon, first sheriff of Logan County, substituted for Tilghman and was placed in charge.

The posse of thirteen men was sworn in, divided, and each

group assigned to one of the two covered wagons in which they would make the trip. They were provisioned with arms, ammunition, food, and a case of good whiskey—in case of snakebite. The lead wagon of the little army and its arsenal left Guthrie on August 31 and was manned by Bat Masterson's brother, U.S. Deputy Marshal Jim Masterson, with W. C. Roberts, Henry Kelly, Hi Thompson, George Cox, H. A. Janson, and Lafe Shadley. Following close behind was the second wagon, driven by Dick Speed. His men were John Hixon, Thomas Hueston, Ike Steel, Red Lucas, and J. S. Burke.

Three of the thirteen possemen were former deputies under U.S. Marshal William Grimes: Dick Speed was at that time city marshal at Perkins; Tom Hueston was serving as city marshal at Stillwater; and Lafe Shadley, who had been a deputy marshal in the Coffeyville area at the time of the Dalton raid, served under Grimes at Pawhuska among the Osage Indians. All were considered good shots.

The two wagons, with all but their drivers concealed by flapping canvas, resembled those of the hundreds of Boomers to be seen in the Territory as the possemen made their way through Langston and Goodnight. They crossed the Cimarron River at Perkins and passed northeast to Ingalls, where they arrived early on the historic morning of September 1, 1893, and pitched camp in a draw southwest of town. The party attracted little, if any, attention, since a large number of homesteaders making preparations for the Cherokee Strip run, slated for September 16, were in the vicinity. In fact, it was estimated that there were several hundred people camped in and around Ingalls awaiting the opening. It might be well to point out that by now the snakebite medicine was being used up at an alarming rate. Nobody had actually been bitten by a snake—but it was always good to be prepared.

Two deputies, Bill Lucas and another, were immediately dispatched into town to get the lay of the land while the rest prepared breakfast. Shortly after 9 A.M., the scouts were back with the report that seven outlaws had just ridden into town and put their horses in Ransom's livery stable, next door to the saloon. Here they left orders to feed and unsaddle the horses, which meant they planned to stay for the day at least. Arkansas Tom, who had been ailing, had gone over to Pierce's O.K. Hotel, where he checked in and went upstairs to bed. Bill Doolin, Bitter Creek Newcomb, Tulsa Jack Blake, Dynamite Dick, Bill Dalton, and Red Buck Weightman all went into Ransom's Saloon. First they lined up at the saloon bar and had drinks all around (except Bill Doolin, who seldom drank), served by bartenders Murray and Myers. After a drink or two, they drifted away to the poker table and began a friendly game. Bitter Creek stood guard, leaning against the bar, watching.

The town's boys would wait around the front of the saloon for the outlaws to ride into town. After they dismounted, the boys would take the horses down to the stable, being paid a quarter or a half-dollar for their services. On their way down to the creek to fish, these same boys would, on occasion, be stopped by the outlaws, who would ask them whether there were any strangers in town. If there were none, the outlaws would ride on into town. If there were, they would turn and ride in another direction after giving the boys several tips.

Old man Chambers was down near the end of the bar drinking himself into a stupor, as was his custom about once every six months. The only other person present at the bar at this early hour was N. A. Walker.

In the meantime, Deputy Hixon had dispatched a messenger to Stillwater to Chief Deputy U.S. Marshal Hale, where he was attending court, with instructions to bring reinforcements. He also ordered his men to prepare for a fight, loaded them into the wagons, and started for Ingalls. Masterson's wagon skirted the south side of town, headed north, and stopped in a grove of trees just north of the home of Dr. J. H. Pickering on the northeast side of town, where the men unloaded and sought shelter behind trees, a hay stack, and some buildings.

Dick Speed drove his wagon north and then east on the section line north of town. As he moved along, his men dropped from the rear of the wagon and took cover behind buildings, fences, and trees on the west side of town. Speed turned his empty wagon south down Ash Street, which was the main street of Ingalls. He passed Light's blacksmith shop on the corner, bringing his team to a halt behind a buggy in the street directly in front of Pierce's livery stable. He got his Winchester and walked into the barn through the double doors, which were open, and there found a boy, twelve-year-old Oscar Wagoner, and Pierce, the owner. He warned them there was to be shooting and that if one or both notified the outlaws, they would be shot down exactly like the outlaws.

Back at the saloon, Joe Chambers had passed out, and Leamon Myers dragged him over into a corner to sober up, as was the custom in his case. Bitter Creek was unaware of the marshal's presence in town, so picked up his Winchester and went next door to the livery stable and saddled his horse. With the gun across the pommel of his saddle, he rode north on Ash Street to visit his lady friend, Sadie Conley, who lived next door to the O.K. Hotel.

Bitter Creek's horse, Old Ben, walked up the street toward Pierce's livery stable. Dick Speed, thinking his presence and mission in town were known, stepped from the livery stable and, resting his rifle across the front wheel of the buggy, took careful aim and fired at Bitter Creek as he rode up the street and just as he came abreast of the town well. Speed's first shot struck Bitter Creek's gun in the middle with a dull thud and whine, smashing the magazine and letting the spring and shell fall to the ground. This rendered Bitter Creek's Winchester useless except as a single-shot rifle. The impact split the bullet, half of it entering Bitter Creek's body near the right groin, clipping off the end of his spinal column. Then it curled back to make its exit near the left groin. The remaining half of the bullet hummed harmlessly off into the distance.

Holding the damaged rifle, Bitter Creek fired once, missing Speed; this was the last of his cartridges, so, shifting the Winchester to his left hand, he drew his Colt with his right hand. He was the fastest and one of the best shots with a revolver in the entire gang. He fired two shots in rapid succession—so fast that most persons hearing the sound thought he had fired only once. His accuracy proclaimed itself as Dick Speed, who had fully exposed himself to finish off the wounded outlaw, took a .45 slug. It entered his left breast and came out of his back just to the right of his spine. He staggered from the impact of the heavy bullet and then pitched forward onto the ground.

Bitter Creek righted himself in the saddle, holstered the Colt, and, gripping the bloody saddle horn with his right hand, wheeled his horse south and dashed wildly down the deserted street, still clutching his useless Winchester in his left hand. As the wounded rider attempted to get away, Deputy Marshal Masterson's men, holed up near Dr. Pickering's place, opened fire and tried to stop the fleeing rider.

Rev. Platt went to the aid of Speed and helped him to the porch of a nearby store. He attempted to give the dying man a drink, but Speed was unable to swallow and died very soon. Thus Deputy Marshal Speed, who had the dubious honor of firing the first shot in the gunfight at Ingalls, was the first to die.

The five outlaws at the poker table scooped up their rifles and dashed outside to see what was going on. As the marshals began shooting, the outlaws all took cover in the saloon and began to return the fire, covering Bitter Creek's flight. And Bitter Creek, not too stable in the saddle and bleeding profusely, made a dash for the open door of Ransom's livery barn, which he made without being hit a second time. He rode at a wild gallop, gripping his Winchester in one hand

and reeling drunkenly in the saddle as he dashed out the rear door of the stable and disappeared down a draw to the southwest.

On his flight out of town, Bitter Creek met a farmer going into Ingalls and stopped him long enough to send a message: "Tell the fellows I'm gone. I've got only a farmer's gun to fight with." He meant he could load only one shell at a time into his Winchester, fire, and load again, since the magazine had been torn away by Speed's bullet.

When the fight started, Dr. Selph, whose office was at that time in the rear of a grocery store, had just amputated a finger for Lew Ferguson, who had smashed it in a threshing machine southwest of town. Another man, Dent Ramsey, was also in the store when the shooting started. There were three empty barrels in the middle of the room and the three men jumped behind these for protection. Dr. Selph, guessing what was going on outside—and to have a little fun of his own— kicked the barrels over and watched the trio scurry for the back door and run to a small ravine some three hundred yards away.

Some small boys were playing marbles in front of the hotel. One of their mothers dashed out into the street, gathered up her son, and hustled the rest to shelter. Mrs. Wagner ran over to her husband's blacksmith shop, despite the gunfire, where she found him hidden behind a pile of scrap iron in the rear of the shop. She insisted that he return to their house.

Dr. Selph lived in a house at the end of the street, and he knew that his wife would be frightened and that if he did not go to her, she would come to him. Being well acquainted with all of the outlaws, he knew they would not shoot him unless by mistake. He also was known to the marshals, but was afraid that if he should run out into the street, he would be mistaken by either side for someone else and would be shot. Therefore, he left the store by the front door and walked briskly up the street in full view of everyone while shots rang out up and down the street. When he arrived at his home, bullets were whistling through the house.

In order to save the baby, Mrs. Selph had put her on the floor and covered her with a feather bed—the doctor was afraid the baby might be smothered. He gathered up his family and hurried to a neighbor's cave, which was already overflowing with men, women, and children, some praying, some shouting, all excited. The doctor stayed only long enough to get his family safely inside, then went back into the street to aid the wounded.

When the fight started, George Ransom, owner of the south saloon and livery stable, was taking a snooze on a pool table in a half-completed shed being built on the south side of his saloon. He jumped to his feet and made a beeline for the front door of the saloon, but before he could get inside, a shot from a rifle where the marshals were stationed hit him in the leg and knocked him down. He managed to drag himself into the saloon and back into the icehouse for protection. Murray joined him shortly, but not until he had been hit in the arm and side. Leamon Myers was the third guest in the icehouse, having escaped there without injury. He later recalled that it sounded like hail was hitting the building as they huddled in the sawdust, ice, and darkness in the small room until the fight was over.

N. A. Walker was still in the saloon. During a lull in the fighting, he made a dash out the front door and was shot down in the street by the marshals. The bullet caught him in the middle and passed through the liver. He folded up and sprawled headlong into the street, where he lay, unable to move, until after the shooting was over. He was finally picked up and carried to the Thomas home, west of the saloon and across the street, and put in a swing on the front porch, where he remained until a doctor could come to his aid. After the battle, he was placed in the front window of the Nix Restaurant, stripped, and left naked in an effort to keep him cool until he could be taken to Stillwater. Small boys of the town walked by and looked at him, for this seemed to be quite a novelty.

Fourteen-year-old Dal Simmons, a student from Duncan Bend, Kansas, visiting in Ingalls was also mortally wounded. He was in the drugstore when the fight began and tried to get away by running across the street to Vaughn's Saloon. He then ran out the back door of the saloon and was mistaken for an outlaw by the marshals, who shot him down as he dashed for cover.

A horse broke loose from the hitching post in front of Selph's store and post office, dashed madly down the vacant street, and was killed by a stray bullet from an unknown gun in front of the drugstore. The animal kicked a few times, then lay motionless. A chicken crossing the street was also killed. The horse continued to lie where it had fallen and gradually began to bloat as blood bubbled from a bullet hole in its side. This was a grim reminder that death stalked the streets of Ingalls that day, and anything that moved was a target for both sides.

Arkansas Tom, who was asleep when the shooting started, was awakened by the rattle of gunfire and soon entered the fracas from his high vantage point in the upstairs room at the hotel. He scooped up his Winchester and dashed to one of the south windows to see what was going on in the street below. He made his shots count. He saw Bitter Creek race madly down the street, covered by fire from the rest of the gang.

Tom had entered the fray with great success, for the marshals had not expected resistance from a sniper upstairs. His fire probably saved Bitter Creek from further injury because the marshals began to direct their fire at the hotel. The marshals were not as well placed as they had hoped to be, for Speed's shot had brought on the fight before they were ready.

When the battle started, Jim Masterson found himself near Dr. Pickering's house behind a blackjack tree that was too small to hide his robust frame. The outlaws were shooting bark off the tree, and bullets were whining all about him. Hixon had taken cover in a shallow ditch and was pumping shot after shot into the saloon at long range. The air was thick with flying lead as both sides opened up with the best they had.

Van Hron, a drummer from Mulhall, had just driven up in front of the hotel when the first shot was fired, and he hastily wheeled his team and disappeared between the hotel and the next house. Old-timers say there was not enough room for a buggy to pass between the buildings, but this one did. Hron beat a hasty retreat over the hills and didn't return for a week.

All of this was happening while Bitter Creek was making his getaway, and by the time he had disappeared into the timber over the next hill, a brief lull had developed. During the lull, the marshals moved in closer and took better cover. Hixon's men moved closer behind the stores and outbuildings from the west and to better cover on the side and rear of the saloon. Meanwhile, Masterson's men moved into the brush and behind the buildings from their positions behind a haystack and some trees near the home of Dr. Pickering, then behind the hotel, then south behind the homes of Drs. Call, Selph, and McCurty. From these vantage points, they were able to shoot to better advantage as they covered the front of Ransom's Saloon and the livery stable.

Feeling more secure, Hixon shouted to Bill Doolin and his gang to come out and surrender or be killed because they were completely surrounded and had no chance of escape. Doolin's answer: "Go to hell!"—punctuated by a hail of hot lead from his .45.

In reply to Doolin's invitation, the marshals opened up on the saloon in earnest, and splinters and chips from the walls of the saloon flew in all directions. The barrage became so heavy that the outlaws decided to make a run for their horses in the barn next door.

Doolin led the escape while the others covered him with a

shower of lead. He dashed into the open door of the barn and opened fire on the marshals as Red Buck and Bill Dalton zigzagged down the plank sidewalk and into the livery barn. The three outlaws joined forces and shot at everything that moved. Tulsa Jack and Dynamite Dick, firing as they ran, made a dash and gained temporary shelter in the barn, both untouched by the marshals' fire.

These sudden, daring moves on the part of the outlaws forced the marshals to shift their positions again in order to cover the livery stable, where the six were again barricaded. Deputy Hueston moved around the corner from behind Perry's store so that he could cover the front door of the barn. In doing so, he exposed himself to the fire of Arkansas Tom, posted at the upstairs window of the hotel. Tom pulled down on Hueston with his Winchester and shot him twice—in the side and bowels—knocking him down in the street just east of the town well, where he lay writhing and twisting in pain.

Lafe Shadley made a run for the livery barn and succeeded in gaining cover behind Dr. Call's house, from which spot he returned the outlaws' fire. All the while it was necessary for the marshals to keep out of the line of fire from both the hotel and the livery barn, since the outlaws had already demonstrated their deadly accuracy from both places.

Inside the barn, Doolin and Dynamite Dick saddled and bridled their horses while Bill Dalton, Tulsa Jack, and Red Buck held off the marshals. Doolin and Dynamite Dick mounted their horses in the barn and, while the others held off the officers, made a wild dash out the rear door and down the draw to the southwest in the same general direction that

Bitter Creek had taken. Dalton, Red Buck, and Tulsa Jack made a wild run out the front door of the stables—against the advice of Doolin. Dalton led the charge, and his horse hit the street in a full gallop. Hixon, guarding the street entrance to the barn, fired at the outlaws as they suddenly appeared on the street. He succeeded in hitting Dalton's horse in the jaw. The animal began spinning around and became unmanageable for a time, but Dalton finally got him started again. He ran the horse about seventy-five yards before Shadley, from his position near Call's house, fired and broke the horse's leg. The beautiful Cleveland Bay was a favorite mount of Dalton's, one he hated very much to lose. As the horse fell, Dalton leaped clear. The horse, however, regained his feet and Dalton walked a short distance on the opposite side of the horse, using it as a shield as it hobbled along on three legs. Dalton finally abandoned the horse and ran south on foot to rejoin the others where they had stopped at a wire fence. Too late they realized that the only pair of wire cutters was in the saddlebags of Dalton's abandoned horse. Dalton then ran back to the horse, under heavy fire, to retrieve the cutters while the other outlaws held the marshals at bay and helped to divert their attention and fire.

Lafe Shadley, in an attempt to gain a better firing position, tried to go through Dr. Call's fence and while doing so was shot by one of the outlaws. He finally made it through the fence to George Ransom's house, where he tried to gain admittance. Mrs. Ransom ordered him to leave and go to the cave where Dr. Selph had taken his family because, she explained, there was a pregnant woman under the bed, screaming and nearly frightened to death. Shadley then staggered to the corner of the house in an attempt to reach the cave. It was there, gun in hand, that Dalton saw him appear at the corner of the house and pumped several shots at him from his Winchester, held waist high. Dalton's shots took deadly effect and Shadley fell to the ground, dropping his beautiful pearl-handled .45 Colt revolver. He was still able to crawl to the cave, however, where those hidden below ground were safe from gunfire.

Dalton retrieved the wire cutters from the saddlebags, shot his injured horse, and ran down to the fence, cut it, and mounted behind one of the other outlaws and they crossed the draw south of town. Here they stopped for a few minutes and fired a number of shots up Oak Street, where Dr. Pickering lived. Frank Briggs, fourteen-year-old son of Dr. Briggs, ran out into the street to look at the departing outlaw band and was hit in the shoulder by a stray bullet from the departing outlaws. It proved to be only a flesh wound.

The acrid smell of gunpowder was everywhere, and a blue haze of gunsmoke drifted lazily in the warm September breeze. All was quiet now. Up to this point, the gun battle had taken less than thirty minutes. Six men had been killed or wounded in the streets of Ingalls that day. It was a deadlier fight than the one at the O.K. Corral at Tombstone, Arizona Territory. Of the outlaws, Bitter Creek was badly wounded in the groin, but the rest escaped unscathed.

At Falls City, two miles southwest of Ingalls, it was an ordinary September morning. Uncle Joe Vickery was in his blacksmith shop sharpening a plowshare at the anvil. Suddenly, from the direction of Ingalls, came the sound of rifle shots, a few at first, then a barrage. Uncle Joe ran out of the shop to have a look around, and Mother Vickery left her kitchen and joined him. The Vickerys did not wait long before they heard the sound of a fast-traveling horse. Soon, horse and rider appeared from the direction of Ingalls. The rider was slumped over the saddle horn. Blood was pouring from wounds in his groin, staining the saddle and the rider's trouser legs a bright crimson, running down over his boots, and dripping onto the ground.

Bill Vickery and S. T. Kirby rode into the yard about the same time Bitter Creek arrived in his blood-soaked condition. Bitter Creek told in a few tense tight-lipped sentences of the fight with the marshals. Bill Vickery and Kirby lit out in a full gallop for Ingalls. Sherman Sanders, who lived across the road, came on the run. Sherm and Uncle Joe helped Bitter Creek off his horse, washed and dressed his wounds, then helped him to remount. Bitter Creek rode off to the east at a fast trot and was soon out of sight.

Arkansas Tom remained in complete command of the hotel and still pumped shot after shot at the marshals. He crept and darted about the room to shoot out of the shattered windows. While the battle was at its hottest, the wash stand-mirror was broken and bullets smashed the pitcher and bowl and splintered the woodwork and door of the room. During the fight, Arkansas Tom sent Alva Pierce, the twelve-year-old son of the hotelkeepers, out to the stable to bring him more ammunition, which was accomplished without incident.

Dr. Pickering dressed Briggs's shoulder, then gave Walker

first aid. Next he went to the Ransom saloon and dressed the wounds of Murray and Ransom. Ransom's arm was in pretty bad shape: the bone had been shattered, and some of the flesh had been shot away. Ransom also had a flesh wound in the side.

The remaining members of the posse surrounded the hotel and demanded that Tom surrender. He refused. At about this time, reinforcements under Deputy Hale arrived from Stillwater and began to bang away at the hotel. Hale informed Tom that he was outnumbered and would eventually be shot. About 1:30 P.M., Tom shouted down to send Dr. Pickering to see him. This was done, and the doctor, accompanied by Alva Pierce and the Wandell boy, went into the hotel and called to Tom but received no answer. Just as the doctor was leaving, Tom called down to ask if it was the doctor. He was told yes and asked if he were hurt. Although he said no, he insisted that the doctor come on up to see him, which Pickering finally did.

Arkansas Tom had taken off his boots and vest, as well as his coat, and was holding his Winchester in his hands. His revolver lay on the bed. The doctor tried to persuade him to give up, but Tom refused. He said that he did not believe he could get justice, which was the reason for his refusal. He did not want to hurt anyone, he said, but would not be taken alive. He wanted to know where the boys were. After being told they had departed in haste, he stated he never would believe that they would have left him. (Doolin later explained that he thought Tom had escaped and that none of the outlaws had intended to desert him.) Tom began to run low on ammunition about 2:00 P.M. He then agreed to surrender to a preacher by the name of Mason, providing he would be protected from the mob and would not be put in chains.

Edith Doolin, five months with child, remained hidden in the hotel throughout the battle and, despite the heavy fire centered there, remained uninjured. She worried about Bill's being captured, but was finally told of his daring escape.

Hale, accompanied by possemen W. C. Roberts and Ike Steel, returned to Guthrie with the prisoner and his horse. Among others taken to Guthrie were John Nix, Sherman Sanders, George Perrin, old man Murray, Mr. and Mrs. George Ransom, two boys named Case from one family, and two boys of the same name belonging to another family. Marshal Nix, however, released one of the boys, Lon Case, whom he recognized and knew not to have been connected in any way with the outlaws. The Ransoms were charged with harboring the outlaws, and the others were held as witnesses, but all were back home in Ingalls within a day or two.

In a second wagon was loaded the dead body of Dick Speed and the wounded Shadley and Hueston, who were rushed to Stillwater for treatment. The others were left in Ingalls. Simmons died at 6:00 P.M., Shadley and Hueston lived three or four days, and Walker, who had been shot through the liver, lingered until the sixteenth of September, when he, too, died.

Deputy Hale and a posse of eleven men followed the trail of the fleeing outlaws. All they were able to find was a place where Bitter Creek had stopped to bathe his wounds— marked by some drying blood on the ground near a stream—

and a spot in a corn field where he had rested for a while. His trail was lost, but the rest of the gang was trailed south to the Cimarron River. After crossing the river, the trail vanished into the Creek Nation, and the posse returned emptyhanded.

After several stops to pour cold water on his wounds, Bitter Creek made it to a small cabin not far south of Ingalls, where he was hidden in a loft by the gang. On several occasions the marshals had ridden by the cabin in their search for him, but did not discover his hiding place. Bill Doolin got Dr. Bland of Cushing, who was at his farm south of Ingalls, to come to the cabin, where he operated on Bitter Creek, using surgical instruments which Doolin had sent a man to borrow from Dr. Pickering. Bitter Creek finally recovered, although the wound was very serious and he had lost a great deal of blood.

After the smoke of battle had cleared away and it had been determined that there were no less than one hundred bullet holes in the Ransom saloon, someone noticed that Joe Chambers was still over in the corner, dead drunk and still asleep. McGinty, thinking it would be a good joke—and as long as he was planning to dress one of the chickens killed in the fight anyway—removed the intestines from a chicken and carefully slid them down the front in the bib of Chambers' overalls. The old man slept peacefully on. After a time, when the bunch could wait no longer to see his reaction, someone woke him up and told him there had been a big fight, with lots of shooting, which he had missed while he slept.

The old man blinked a few times, like a toad during a hailstorm, in trying to comprehend the situation and finally, after a couple of tries, got to his feet, wobbling. Just about then he discovered the chicken entrails in his overalls. He slowly paled as he gently thrust his hand down the front of the bib. He hesitated for a moment, then shouted in a hoarse voice, "My God, all of my guts have been shot out!" It was said that the old man never took another drink.

Dr. Pickering found a number of unfired cartridges near the marshals' hiding place, where, in their haste and confusion, they had merely pumped the shells through the rifles without firing them. Mrs. Ransom found Shadley's beautiful Colt .45 (a single-action Army Model, 4.5-inch barrel, nickel-plated, ivory-handled weapon, serial no. 97445) lying near the corner of the house, where it had fallen when he was shot the last time. She picked it up, folded it in her apron, and took it into the house, where she put it in the top of a trunk for safe-keeping. In a day or two, the same gun found its way to the home of Mrs. Williams, stepdaughter of George Ransom, west of town. She carefully wrapped it up and hid it in a hollow log near the ceiling of her homestead cabin.

Bill Wilson took the hand-tooled, silver-mounted saddle off Dalton's dead horse and hid it under a wagon. In a few days, Dalton was using his saddle again. Doolin later asked Dalton why he had deliberately gunned Shadley down with his Winchester. "The dirty son of a bitch should have shot me instead of my favorite saddle horse," Dalton replied.

The fight at Ingalls was the most desperate and exciting gun battle between organized banditry and peace officers in the Southwest, or even in the Old West. When the smoke had cleared from the bloody battlefield, ten more names were added to the pages of American folklore: Bill Doolin, Arkansas Tom Daugherty, Bill Dalton, Bitter Creek Newcomb, Tulsa Jack Blake, Dynamite Dick Clifton, Red Buck Weightman, Lafe Shadley, Dick Speed, and Tom Hueston.

7

THE AFTERMATH OF THE INGALLS BATTLE

HISTORIANS ARE IN GENERAL AGREEMENT that the battle at Ingalls was the beginning of the end for Doolin's gang, as well as the other organized groups of outlaws and freebooters in both Oklahoma Territory and Indian Territory. The pressure of public sentiment, as well as that of the bankers' association, the railroads, and Wells, Fargo Express, was being felt all the way from top officials in Washington to those in the lowest ranks among the peace officers. To put the final touch to the whole affair, large rewards were being posted for the outlaws "dead or alive," which gave every man among the citizenry an incentive to get into the act. It was now legal to bushwhack an outlaw who was wanted by the sheriff or marshals and still receive the reward. This led to a number of killings in cold blood, but accomplished its aim in exterminating the outlaws.

A report was out on September 12 that Doolin and his gang were intending to rescue Arkansas Tom from the federal bastile at Guthrie, and a heavy guard was posted around the building. Doolin failed to show up. Tom remained in jail until April, 1894, at which time, chained and under heavy guard, he was taken before Judge Frank Dale at Stillwater and arraigned for the murder of Hueston, Shadley, and Speed. He was tried at the court's May term, convicted of murdering Tom Hueston, and sentenced to fifty years at hard labor in the prison at Lansing, Kansas.

During the trial, Heck Thomas and eight or nine other deputy marshals had been stationed as guards because Doolin was still expected to make good his threat to take Tom by force. Everyone who entered the courthouse was carefully searched for concealed weapons. However, nothing happened.

After the sentencing, Judge Dale called Marshal E. D. Nix into his chambers and told him that in view of the evidence presented in the case, he felt that in the future it would be better to bring the outlaws in dead, if necessary, and to stop trying to bring them in alive at the risk of peace officers' lives —too many were being wiped out. For Doolin, it was another deadly blow.

The order was put into action and brought on the greatest manhunt ever staged in the Southwest. Nix, who was territorial marshal at this time, directed the hunt. The cleanup, however, was left in the hands of his successor, Pat Nagle, who was in office at the time Bill Doolin and several other members of the gang were killed. Most of the plans for capturing and/or eradicating the outlaws came under the direction of Tilghman, Madsen, and Thomas, who did the actual work in the field. It is also quite possible that Marshal Frank Canton of Pawnee would have eventually brought Doolin in for the reward money, dead or alive, if given a little more time and if he had not been operating at a disadvantage by competing with the Guthrie marshals, who had the squeeze play on the available informers. The marshals had a cattle stealing charge against the Dunn brothers. This was held over the Dunns' heads, with a promise of dismissal if they would inform the Guthrie office of Doolin's movements.

The marshals did not have time to look for Doolin and his boys; they were too busy preparing for the Cherokee Strip opening on September 16, 1893. Doolin and Dynamite Dick spent a few days in Alfred (Mulhall) after the Ingalls battle, boarding their horses in John Hron's livery stable. They soon drifted back over into Payne County, however, to make plans for a new raid. Their funds were getting low. Doolin and the others, with the exception of Bill Dalton, stayed in the Ingalls area, spending a good part of their time at the Dunns'.

A practice that failed to endear the territorial marshals to people in general was planting liquor in farmers' wagons while the latter were in town doing their trading. The farmers were then arrested and the planted stuff used as evidence. So one can see there were bitter feelings toward the deputy marshals, who were paid fees for arrests and mileage but no regular salary. At the Strip opening, Nix appointed one thousand special deputies. Quite a number of these men made the run, although they were ineligible to do so. There were, of course, many honest marshals, but people couldn't be sure at first glance which kind they were dealing with.

Doolin and his boys were openly frequenting their old haunts again by mid-October. On one Saturday of that month, Doolin and Dalton walked the streets of Stillwater like any other citizens. Doolin kept himself a little more scarce and stopped indoors, but Dalton walked around more boldly— dressed in a fine suit of citizen's clothes. They came in on Friday night, put up at a house, and stayed in the city all day

Saturday. The two let it be known that they had come to wing Doc Roberts and Charley Marx because Roberts had played spy on the gang at Ingalls. They wanted Deputy Marshal Marx because he had made it so hot for them in the Osage country. Two other desperados were now riding regularly with the gang: Charlie Pierce and Tulsa Jack Blake.

Chris Madsen got word that Doolin and his boys were hiding at Dave and Jerry Fitzgerald's horse ranch in Pleasant Valley. The bachelor brothers had come to the Indian country in the 1880s and had a reputation for harboring outlaws. Dave had homesteaded a farm when Oklahoma Territory was opened for settlement, building a half-dugout.

Madsen put together a small posse and rode out to the Fitzgerald's place. He demanded to know where the outlaws were and accused Dave of harboring them. This the Fitzgeralds denied, but stated that "a man has to feed a person who stops by." Chris berated Dave further and was told that if he was so all-fired anxious to capture Doolin and his gang, they were hiding in the willows down by the creek. Chris was no fool, and he knew that he and his four deputies would have no chance against outlaws who were already holed up. He wheeled his horse, led his posse out of the yard, and faded fast into the distance. He would fight another day on a battlefield of his own choosing.

One of Doolin's eating places when he was on the dodge was Charley Burns's hotel in Clayton, located on the north side of the Cimarron River west of Ripley. He would ride up to the back of the hotel and tie his horse to a tree near the door, never unsaddling the animal. It was his custom to sit on the side of the round oak dining table facing the door. He would place his Winchester across his knees and out of sight and his six-gun at his hip. Della Burns served the patrons and would be on duty the morning the marshals drove through town with Doolin's body.

Sometimes Doolin would stop off at the store in Clayton and visit with the storekeeper. He often sat there and read from the newspapers about the exploits of Bill Doolin, giving the details from memory and not depending on the printed page. On one occasion, he left a huge roll of bills, tied with a string, with the storekeeper with instructions that in the event his death were reported, the man was to go and see for himself whether Doolin were really dead. If so, he was to bury Doolin and send the balance of the money to Doolin's sister in Arkansas. The money was hidden on a shelf behind some groceries, but in a week or so Doolin returned and asked for the money—to the great relief of the storekeeper.

One night Van Hron of Mulhall checked into a small hotel in Payne County and was given the last available room. Someone knocked at the front door of the hotel and the landlord asked, "Who's there and what do you want?" It was Bill Doolin and he needed a night's lodging. When he was informed that the house was full, Doolin inquired who was in No. 3. When told that it was Van Hron, he said, "I'll share Van's bed." Van took the back side of the bed after pulling it out from the wall. Doolin asked him why he had done this. Van replied that if there should be any shooting, he wanted to roll over behind the bed for protection.

On November 16, 1893, Bill Doolin and Dynamite Dick held up a Mr. Higginbotham at Blackwell. The two pulled down on him with their Winchesters, demanding his money. He told them that two dollars was all he had, and Bill Doolin took one of the dollars with the remark: "There is nothing small about me; you keep the other dollar." He then bade Higginbotham to be on his way and he and his partner rode off.

Early in December, Doolin went into Ingalls and picked up his wife at the O.K. Hotel, where she had been working for some time. She was eight-months pregnant, and he wanted her to go to a safe place for their child to be born. He loaded her and their meager belongings into a wagon and drove to Chandler, where they boarded with a family he knew. Now Chandler was the home of Bill Tilghman, who had a farm there and raised fine race horses. Doolin made it a point not to run into Tilghman during his stay in town.

In the late afternoon of January 5, 1894, Bill Doolin and one of his henchmen entered the post office at Clarkson in Payne County, just north of Pleasant Valley in Logan County, Oklahoma Territory, held up the postmaster, Waltman, and looted the office of all the registered mail and money on hand. They fled in the general direction of Stillwater.

Doolin was low on funds and planned a bank robbery at Pawnee. Bitter Creek had now recovered from his wounds enough to ride and use a gun. On January 28, Doolin, Bitter Creek, and Tulsa Jack rode to a spot near Pawnee and made camp outside town, as many others were doing, so they would not be noticed by anyone. Tulsa Jack went into town and scouted the bank during the afternoon, and he and Bitter Creek put on their slickers and rode into town again after dark and bought some corn for their horses from Bill Mc-Ginty, who was operating a livery stable with a man by the name of Birch. McGinty thought he recognized them, but was not sure. The next day, a Tuesday, about 4:00 P.M. the three men rode up to the Farmers and Citizens Bank at the northeast corner of the square. Doolin and Tulsa Jack dismounted, leaving Bitter Creek with the horses, and proceeded to the bank. Bill Doolin had selected the time carefully: it was shortly before closing time and it would soon be dark. Pursuit would be much more difficult at night.

They held the cashier, C. L. Berry, at gunpoint, and ordered him to open the safe. Tulsa Jack covered the only customer in the bank while Doolin stepped behind the counter. Berry made a frantic effort to open the safe, but the time lock was set, as they learned a little later, and the door would not open. Doolin put his gun to Berry's head and said: "Fail on that job again and I'll blow your brains out." Berry tried again, but explained that the safe could not be opened until the time for which the lock was set. Doolin put his ear to the safe. Hearing the timer running, he was satisfied that Berry was telling the truth. He then gathered up about $300 from the teller's change drawer and marched the frightened cashier out the front door to the place where Bitter Creek was waiting with the horses. They mounted, and Doolin ordered Berry up behind him so he could be used as a shield as they rode madly down the street. They fired a volley of shots into the front of Bolton's meat market, where several citizens had taken cover.

Tulsa Jack shot down the sign on the market. He had lost his hat, but he didn't pause to retrieve it.

When they crossed Black Bear Creek, Doolin ordered Berry to "pile off," which he did without ceremony and started walking back to town, but not until Tulsa Jack had taken his cap and put it on his own head. He told the banker that he would trade him the hat he had left at the bank for the cap. The outlaw's hat was kept on display in the bank for a number of years.

A short distance out of town, Sheriff Frank Lake and Chief Deputy Frank Canton met Berry walking back to Pawnee. A posse was soon formed by the sheriff and took off in hot pursuit of the outlaws. A few miles south of town, they found signs on a hillside where the gang had stopped to rest a while before going on. The trail was lost in the darkness at Gray Horse Ford. Doolin and his boys had successfully pulled their second bank robbery.

The gang rode north, then swung east and south to return to Ingalls. Doolin rode over to Chandler to be with his wife and newborn son. About the first of March, he moved his family to Edith's father's place at Lawson. From here he planned his next move. It was based on a dispatch sent from Leavenworth, Kansas, and published in the *Kansas City Times* on Saturday morning, March 10, 1894. How the *Times* got the secret information was never learned. The dispatch stated the intended movements of the U.S. Army paymaster, the amount of money going to each post, and by what means of transportation it was to be taken there. Doolin and Bill Dalton planned the robbery.

On the cold windy morning of March 13, Doolin and Dalton entered the railroad hotel at Woodward and went upstairs to the rooms of the station agent, George W. Rourke. They awakened him with the gentle nudge of a pistol and told him to dress quietly. Then they marched him downstairs and over to the depot. As they approached, they saw a young man named Sam Peters lounging near the baggage room. He was ordered to fall in and put up his hands.

Inside the office, they forced Rourke to open the safe and sack up $6,540 in currency consigned to the army paymaster at nearby Fort Supply. The express company was responsible for the money and the U.S. government did not foot the loss. Doolin and Dalton then forced Rourke and Peters to carry the small way safe a quarter of a mile east of the station, where they forced it open, looted the contents, and left the safe lying open on the ground. With their captives, the outlaws proceeded to the stockyards, half a mile east of the depot, where they tied up Peters and Rourke, mounted their horses, which were hidden there, and rode southwest. The victims were discovered at daylight and related their story. A posse was organized at once by Chris Madsen and Sheriff Lake, who was also a deputy marshal.

Largely through his own efforts, Marshal Nix was able to persuade the Department of Justice to offer rewards for territorial outlaws, dead or alive. He also made provisions for adequate pay to possemen enlisted by marshals to run the outlaws down. The War Department, by order of Colonel Parker, commanding officer at Fort Supply, ordered Lieutenant Kirby Walker and twenty cavalrymen, with the aid of

Amos Chapman, veteran Indian scout, to trail and capture the bandit gang.

The scouts hit the trail at daylight and followed it for a short distance to a point where six other riders joined Doolin and Dalton. The six were believed to be Little Dick West, Bitter Creek Newcomb, Charlie Pierce, Dynamite Dick, Bill Raidler, and Red Buck. The posse obtained fresh horses at Moss Zeigler's ranch and continued in hot pursuit, but the outlaws vanished into the canyons and gulches of the badlands in the Cheyenne country.

Bill Tilghman finally got wind of the fact that Lafe Shadley's gun was at the Williams place, so he made a special trip to get it, if possible. Mrs. Williams answered his knock. Tilghman explained that he was in the process of closing Shadley's estate and understood she might know the whereabouts of his missing gun. She asked what sort of a gun he had in mind, and Tilghman gave her a good description of a gun, but not the one she had hidden in the hollow log of the cabin. She informed Bill she had seen no such gun, which was the truth, so the gun was not recovered at this time.

George Ransom finally came after the gun Mrs. Williams had hidden and took it into town to his saloon. Here Bill Doolin saw it behind the bar and wanted to trade his Colt for it and pay some boot. A trade was finally made, and Doolin owned Shadley's fancy .45 until Tilghman took it from him at Eureka Springs, Arkansas. The gun Doolin traded to Ransom, greatly treasured by him, was finally stolen from the bunkhouse at the Ransom place and was never recovered.

One night Doolin stopped off at the 3D Ranch, owned by a man named Freeman, near Hominy, about thirty-five miles from Tulsa. Freeman's little daughter was sick and needed medical attention, but the nearest physician was Dr. S. G. Kennedy in Tulsa. The only way he could be reached was for someone to go by horseback for him, and the only person free to go for the doctor was Freeman himself. Doolin was waiting for his supper, so he said, "I'll go for the doctor, Freeman. You're needed here with the little girl." So Doolin rode all the way to Tulsa, picked up the doctor, and accompanied him back to the ranch. It was nearly morning when they arrived, and Doolin noticed several mounted men close to the house. "I don't believe I need to go any farther with you," he said to the doctor. "I am Bill Doolin, and those men may be looking for me." And with a nod, he rode off.

Bill Doolin, as well as most of the other outlaws in the Territory, were on friendly terms with a Dr. Charles Wynn of Fairland, Indian Territory, who posed as a cancer doctor. He treated many wounded and ill outlaws as a sideline, and on more than one occasion, he had been known to act as a scout for outlaws who needed a man above suspicion to accept a call to case a bank or express office.

So it was Dr. Wynn who cased the bank at Bentonville, Arkansas, for Henry Starr and Kid Wilson a few days before Starr's gang robbed it on Monday, May 6, 1893. Wynn had been in and out of town frequently for a few weeks prior to the holdup and was in town on the day of the robbery, posing as an innocent bystander. Soon after the robbers had departed, however, the authorities placed him in custody and questioned him. He was a smart fellow and they were unable to connect him with the robbery, so he was released. Henry Starr and his boys got several thousand dollars, most of which was recovered in Colorado Springs, Colorado, where Starr and Wilson were arrested for the crime.

Doolin had been in touch with Dr. Wynn for some time and had commissioned him to case the bank at Southwest City, Missouri. When Doolin had word that all was ready to go, he gathered up six of his best men: Bitter Creek Newcomb, Dick West, Charlie Pierce, Bill Raidler, Bill Dalton, and Dynamite Dick.

The bank so carefully selected was the Southwest City Bank. Southwest City, in McDonald County, Missouri, was located in the extreme southwest corner of Missouri, with the Arkansas line on the south and Indian Territory forming the western city limits. Located on the banks of Honey Creek, a crystal-clear mountain stream with good fishing, the town basked in the May sunshine, unaware of any designs on its business life. Doolin and his gang spent the night at Dr. Wynn's home in Fairland, and on the morning of May 10, 1894, they saddled up and, with Dr. Wynn, leisurely made their way toward Southwest City. As they neared Southwest City, they sent the doctor ahead to scout out the town. He soon was able to report that all was well, so they rode on into town, leaving Dr. Wynn to return to his home where they planned to meet him again that night.

Promptly at 3:00 P.M., the seven jogged up Main Street as if they were just travelers riding through. Doolin, Dalton, and Bitter Creek went directly to the bank, and the remaining four took up positions outside, two in a poolroom just north of and across the street from the post office and the other two in the yard of a Dr. Nichols. With oaths and curses, they ordered everyone to seek cover and began firing their six-guns.

Doolin and his two aides entered the bank and cornered Mr. Ault, owner of the bank, and Mr. Snyder, the cashier. Doolin and Dalton crawled through the cashier's cage while Bitter Creek covered Ault and Snyder. After emptying the open vault and the cashier's drawer of cash, they deposited the money in a grain sack and made for their horses while the outlaws outside kept up their fire. When Doolin and Dalton reached the sidewalk, they met a hail of bullets coming from such weapons as the hill people could get their hands on when they learned the bank was being robbed.

It was at this point that former Senator J. C. Seaborn and his brother Oscar came out of Mrs. Dustin's hardware store to see what was going on. All of the outlaws were mounted by this time and headed west out of town, but as they passed the hardware store, Little Dick West, with a blazing six-gun in each hand, fired at those on the sidewalk who seemed likely to offer resistance. He took a potshot at Oscar Seaborn, who was the best target. The bullet struck Oscar in the lower body, passing through and lodging in the lower abdomen of J. C., who was directly behind him. J. C. died a few days later, but Oscar recovered.

Across the street, an upstairs window was thrown open and a shotgun roared. Buckshot peppered the gang, one of the shots striking Bill Doolin in the left temple near the hairline, nearly knocking him from the saddle. As the blood gushed forth, he was almost blinded by it, but, still firing his gun, he led the gang out of town with the posse not far behind. A man by the name of M. V. Hembre was in the Baker Saloon, and as the gang rode by, he was struck in the ankle by a bullet fired by one of the outlaws. It severed his foot.

Bill Doolin's favorite horse, Old Dick, was struck in the neck with a part of the charge of buckshot meant for his master. After the wound healed, the horse was unable to hold his head erect and was no longer of value as a saddle mount. Dr. Selph at Ingalls bought the animal, and it was driven for years hitched to a cart. Dr. Selph also carried a large, open-faced watch, a gift from Doolin, one he had no doubt stolen in a holdup somewhere.

As the bandits proceeded west, they met Deputy U.S. Marshal Simpson Melton and fired three shots at him, wounding him in the leg. Melton returned the fire, hitting one of the outlaws' horses. In all, about one hundred shots were fired on Main Street during the holdup, which, the bank reported, netted the outlaws $3,700.

As Doolin and his men turned south on Broadway, they met a warm reception from City Marshal Carlyle and several men. Another of the horses was hit by a shot from J. D. Powell, but the superior mounts of the outlaws soon outdistanced the posse. All of Doolin's men were wounded except one, but none of the wounds proved fatal. The outlaws went first to Dr. Wynn's in Fairland, where he patched them up and received his fee for services rendered—both kinds.

Then they proceeded southwest, stopped and fed their horses and ate supper at a farmhouse, then moved on to camp near Grand River for the night.

The bank job had not gone off as smoothly as those at Spearville and Pawnee. In fact, it was a near repeat of the Coffeyville slaying of the Dalton gang. The next day, they crossed the Cherokee and Creek Nations back into Oklahoma Territory (Old Oklahoma), where they were soon hidden away in the Pawnee country. Dr. Wynn was arrested and brought to Southwest City, where he was charged with aiding and abetting bank robbery. He had an alibi, however, and was finally turned loose.

This was Doolin's one and only crime in Missouri. Upon the death of J. C. Seaborn, the governor immediately posted a reward of $500, dead or alive, for any member of Doolin's gang.

Doolin left a message for his son, Jay, with a farmer who lived south of Ingalls and with whom he had once hidden out when he was hard pressed. The message was that should he, Doolin, be killed and buried in a pauper's grave (boot hill), Jay, as soon as he was grown, was to have his father's body moved, for Bill had a horror of being buried in such a place. Jay was never able to carry out his father's request, so Bill Doolin's body remains in a boot hill grave. However, it does have the finest marker in that section of the cemetery.

The bullet wound in Doolin's head was not considered serious, since it finally healed, but as time went on it began to bother him. He had terrible headaches, perhaps because of the buckshot in his head. Several doctors offered to remove it from his skull, where it was believed to be lodged against the brain and causing pressure, but Doolin would not give his consent to the operation. He feared some enterprising doctor might decide to collect the $5,000 reward, which read "dead or alive." So he carried the souvenir from Southwest City to his death, but not to his grave.

In 1893, the marshal's office in Guthrie sent a letter to Bill Doolin asking him to give up and stand trial. This was before some of Doolin's major crimes. He did not call at the post office, however, until the day after the letter was returned, uncalled for, to the marshal's office. Deputy Tilghman urged Mrs. Doolin, then known as Miss Ellsworth, to take the letter to Doolin and ask that he give himself up, but this was not done. Neither of the marshal's efforts counted for anything as far as Doolin was concerned.

On May 23, 1894, Bill Dalton, who had decided to try it on his own, and three other outlaws robbed the First National Bank of Longview, Texas, and fled to the Chickasaw Nation. The desperados divided the money and went their separate ways. Deputy Moss Hart and a posse tracked Dalton to a farmhouse near Elk, twenty-five miles northwest of Ardmore, and surrounded the house on the morning of June 8. Bill was shot and killed as he jumped through a window in a vain effort to escape.

Doolin, upon receiving word that his lieutenant was dead, and with his right-hand man, Arkansas Tom, in the pen, wondered when his number might come up and the marshals get lucky. But it was not yet his time to go. In June, a horse, buggy, and harness were stolen from A. E. McKellap at

Sapulpa, and the stolen property was traced toward the Cherokee Strip by Deputy Marshal Harris and a posse from Fort Smith. Near Cushing, they met Bill Doolin in the buggy, to which was hitched McKellap's horse, with another horse tied behind. Doolin laid his whip to the horse, which proved to be a good one, and held the lead for six miles during a constant running fire kept up by both sides. The rest of the posse was not as well mounted as Harris and gradually fell behind. At a bend in the road, a lucky shot disabled Doolin's horse, so he took to the brush, making good his escape. In the captured buggy were found five hundred rounds of pistol and rifle cartridges. Doolin had not stolen the buggy, but had bought it from the man who did.

Marshal Nix gave orders to arrest all persons in the Territory known to be harboring Doolin or his boys, in the hope that he could break down some of Doolin's friends and get them to inform on him. In January, 1895, Nix ordered Bill Tilghman, Deputy Neal Brown, and Charlie Bearclaw, a former U.S. Army scout, into the Ingalls area to start the ball rolling. They left Guthrie in a covered wagon loaded with camping equipment and supplies to last a month, with saddle horses tied to the endgate. They looked like everyday travelers moving through the country. The second day out, the weather turned bitter cold and it began to snow and sleet. The clouds were a leaden gray, and by midafternoon it was almost dark.

Bearclaw sat hunched up on the seat as the wagon bumped and rumbled over the frozen ground and the snow and sleet beat harshly against his face. Brown and Tilghman rode in the wagon box under the flapping canvas, partly sheltered from the raging prairie storm. They were in the area south of Ingalls on the Dunn farm when they spotted smoke coming out of the chimney of a dugout in a draw. Tilghman decided that they should seek its shelter for the night.

Tilghman got stiffly down from the wagon and trudged through the snow to the dugout, making a mental note that there were no horses or men in view. He banged on the door but received no response. He pushed the unlocked door open and stepped inside. There was a large fireplace on the far wall, and upon the hearth roared a huge fire of blackjack logs. Bill Dunn sat before the fire with a Winchester across his knees. He looked up questioningly but remained silent. There were tiers of bunks on each side of the extra-large room, overhung and hidden from view with quilts and blankets. There were sleeping accommodations for more than a dozen men.

Bill Tilghman had discovered the famous "Rock Fort" of the Dunn brothers, where they were in the habit of harboring outlaws from all over the Territory. Behind the screen of blankets were hidden Bill Doolin, Little Dick West, Red Buck Weightman, Tulsa Jack Blake, Dynamite Dick Clifton, Charlie Pierce, Bitter Creek Newcomb, and Little Bill Raidler, each with a Winchester trained on Tilghman. Recognizing him as he stepped down from the wagon and walked toward the dugout, they had immediately gone into hiding in the bunks. There was no time to get outside and besides, they had him outnumbered.

As Tilghman moved over to warm himself by the fire, he observed the eight rifles covering him from the bunks. He never let on but made some idle conversation with the ranch-man and said he guessed he had better be on his way to Pawnee. He moved over to the door and out into the darkness.

As soon as Tilghman went through the door, Red Buck leaped from his bunk and made a dash for the door to shoot him in the back, but Doolin and Dunn restrained him. Doolin told them that if they killed the ever popular Tilghman, they would have a hundred men down on them by morning and the dugout would be dynamited off the map. The outlaws also decided that the marshals would return with a posse, so they decided to move, despite the bitterness of the weather.

Tilghman did return with a posse, but the chickens had flown the coop. He was, however, able to make a deal with Bill Dunn to be an informer in return for dismissing old charges, appointing Dunn a deputy marshal to share in any rewards, and not pressing charges of harboring outlaws.

For months Doolin had leased a large pasture from the government in the Wichita Mountains Reservation. There, several hundred stolen horses and cattle were herded by the outlaws. One of the Indian police discovered what was going on, but was caught and killed. This forced the gang into hiding deep in the Wichita Mountains. So things rocked along until the spring of 1895, when funds began to run low. It was decided to try another train robbery in order to replenish their cash on hand.

One by one, the gang assembled at a ranch near Dover, remaining there for several days while planning the train holdup. The arrangements for the hideout had been made several days earlier by Whiskey John. Dover, on the Rock Island Railroad, was selected because it was known that the railroad hauled the Army payroll for Texas troops. A tip told the outlaws when to expect the money: April 3, 1895, at 11:45 P.M.

When the train pulled into Dover, Dynamite Dick and Little Dick West boarded the coal tender, and as the train pulled out of the station, they covered the engineer and the fireman with their Winchesters and ordered them to stop the train at the cut a mile south of town. As the train came to a stop, Charlie Pierce, Tulsa Jack, Bitter Creek, Zip Wyatt, Red Buck, and Bill Doolin covered the train from the top of the embankment. They fired a few shots to keep the passengers in the cars and approached the express car. The messenger, Jones by name, closed and locked the doors, and the bandits opened fire at once. About twenty rifle shots crashed through the windows and wooden sides of the express car. Jones was hit in the left leg, and his right wrist and arm were shattered by a bullet before he finally opened the door and gave up.

The way safe had been locked in Kansas City and could be opened only by the express agent in Fort Worth. The fireman and engineer were ordered by the bandits to drill a hole in the safe. They went to work, but had little luck. It was reported, however, that the bandits finally made off with $35,000 from the express car. After thirty minutes of effort, the safe was still locked, so the bandits, becoming nervous, decided to abandon it.

Meanwhile, Zip Wyatt and Charlie Pierce, who had been

sent forward to keep the passengers in line, rounded up the Negro porter and equipped him with a grain sack. They ordered him down the aisle of the cars to collect all the wallets, watches, and jewelry that the passengers had. Zip Wyatt walked close behind the porter with a gun in his back, while Pierce walked backward, covering the rear, to guard against attack from that quarter.

Former U.S. Marshal William Grimes was a passenger in one of the cars, and Zip Wyatt recognized him and ordered him to cough up the dough. Grimes had already hidden his watch under the stove, so he cheerfully tossed $1.40 in small change into the open sack. A goodly number of watches and considerable cash was donated during the forced march and the forced cause. Before leaving the car, Zip Wyatt sent his regards to Chris Madsen by Grimes.

The bandits ordered the engine crew back to the locomotive and told them not to move the train until they heard a shot, which was not long in coming. The train then pulled out for Kingfisher, where the robbery was reported and a posse put together. A report was wired to Chris Madsen's office in El Reno, and when the 3:00 A.M. train headed north for Dover, Madsen and nine deputies were on board with a boxcar hooked on behind the passenger train for the posse's horses.

Madsen and his men arrived in Dover at dawn and were joined there by William Bank and a man named Prater. The outlaws' trail led west for several miles, then turned northwest. The posse followed all morning and at noon arrived at Hail Creek, in Major County near Ames, about twenty miles from Dover. The gang had stopped here for breakfast at a farmhouse. Chris Madsen and his men ate dinner at the same place, then pushed on. Chris divided his men, with his own group heading west and circulating along the Cimarron to see that the gang didn't double back.

Deputy Banks led the second posse and followed a trail that the outlaws did not try to hide. At 2:00 P.M., while trailing the gang through the sandhills, they topped a small knoll, and below, in a small patch of timber, were the outlaws with their horses. They were all asleep except Tulsa Jack, who was standing guard. He saw the possemen as they broke the skyline and fired a shot to warn his sleeping companions. Instantly all were on their feet, but quickly got down when they saw their danger. Deputy Banks aimed with his Winchester and fired, killing Tulsa Jack on the spot. The other members of the gang opened up on the marshals. A couple of hundred shots were fired in the pitched battle, which lasted about three-quarters of an hour. Two of the outlaws' horses were killed, and the gang decided they had better make a run for it, with two of them on one horse, leaving Tulsa Jack where he had fallen. None of the possemen was injured, and none could identify the dead outlaw. Banks and Prater secured a spring wagon and took the body to Hennessey for identification and to collect the reward money.

Deputy Madsen and the remainder of the posse continued to follow the outlaws' trail. A dead horse, the one Doolin had been riding, was found. This had forced another horse to carry double, which would slow their escape. Madsen stayed with the trail, and on the morning of April 6, he came to the farm of an elderly Baptist preacher named Godfrey. The

COLLEGE OF THE SEQUOIAS
LIBRARY

outlaws had arrived at Godfrey's place earlier that morning in search of fresh mounts, for their overloaded horses were worn out. They rode into Godfrey's yard, four men on two horses, while Godfrey was sitting in a rocker on his front porch. Bitter Creek told him what had happen and informed him they were taking his team, "No, boys, you can't have it," said Godfrey.

"Old man, we don't want to hurt you, but we are going to take the team," Bitter Creek threatened. He told Charlie Pierce to dismount and take Godfrey's horses. Charlie started walking toward the horse lot. Godfrey picked up his shotgun, whereupon either Bitter Creek or Red Buck immediately shot him, the bullet striking Godfrey in the head and killing him instantly. (Western historians are not in agreement concerning which of the two outlaws shot Godfrey, but do agree that it was one of them.) They took the horses, and all traveled west toward Canton.

Doolin felt that, with all the heat on them, it was best to divide the train loot and separate to throw off the posses. Each man was given his share, and Bitter Creek, Charlie Pierce, and Red Buck rode off together, shaking the posse in the Glass Mountains, where it was impossible for Chris Madsen to track them. They headed east for the Dunn farm. Red Buck separated from the other two when he learned where they planned to go. He didn't trust the Dunns and was afraid they might be tempted to collect the reward money. Little Bill Raidler went into hiding at the Moore Ranch on Mission Creek in the Osage Nation; Zip Wyatt returned to the Watonga-Okeene area to hole up.

8

THE HANDWRITING ON THE WALL

DOOLIN WAS AWARE that the desperados' latest holdup and the unfortunate killing of Godfrey would receive special attention from the marshal's office, as had already been demonstrated by the slaying of Tulsa Jack and the posse's hot pursuit. Early in the 1890s, Doolin had visited Alma, New Mexico, looking for a ranch job. He had also visited New Mexico on other occasions with the Dalton boys. He felt that the area would be an ideal hideout for a while until the search for them had cooled off. Doolin, Dynamite Dick, and Little Dick West made a beeline for Alma after shaking the posse, who expected them to drift back into the Ingalls area.

After days of hard riding, they arrived at the Rhodes Ranch, located in the San Andres Mountains, the wildest and most isolated section of New Mexico. The town of Alma was known from Canada to the Gulf of Mexico as "the outlaw paradise." When it got too hot for outlaws, they stayed at the ranch of Eugene Manlove Rhodes, the noted western author, and waited out the storm. The ranch was conveniently located for a hideout, with a good getaway exit. Outlaws could go south to the lower end of Socorro County, whose bootheel-shaped lower end joined Sierra, Dona Ana, Otero, and Lincoln counties. Flight could be extended into any one of these counties. If Gene Rhodes knew of the outlaws' presence at the ranch, he put them to work to earn their board and keep. To oppose them would have been foolhardy. With getaway horses always saddled, they did their work as cowboys until warned of an approaching posse. When they left Gene, he was in no position to say which way they had departed.

On the way out to New Mexico, Doolin had bought—not stolen, because he didn't want the law to be looking for him in New Mexico—a big, unbroken, smoky-blue outlaw horse which he felt would make an excellent getaway horse, if he could be broken. He led this animal into the rough back pasture of the ranch where the three outlaws had set up a permanent camp. Dynamite Dick rested up for a week, then decided he would drift over into Arizona for a spell. He hid out at a sheep ranch with a couple of Mexican sheepherders for a while. They finally had a falling out, and he killed and robbed them and headed for Oklahoma and his mother's home near Pauls Valley.

After a couple of weeks, the camp food began to run low, and Doolin decided to ride into Engle for supplies and see if he could find someone to break his blue horse. He had been a good bronco rider in his time, but the wound in his foot and, especially, the buckshot in his head were giving him constant trouble and had slowed him down until he felt that he was no match for Old Blue, as he named the horse. The people of Engle had an answer for Doolin's request for someone to break Old Blue: Gene Rhodes. A rider set out at once to bring Gene, for the whole town wanted to see the show. Gene came back with the messenger; he needed money for riding the horse, and he had no objections to putting on a show for the people of Engle.

By the time Gene arrived, the townspeople were gathered at the corral, ready for the show. Gene looked the horse over carefully and noted that the big bluish-gray "grulla" had very powerful forequarters and a mean head. He was a terrific horse—if he could be broken, one that would carry a man a long way, and fast if necessity demanded. The stranger who owned the horse stood quietly by himself to one side of the crowd with his hat pulled down over his eyes. Gene wondered who he was. "Mr. Hawkins" was the introduction, but Gene was sure that wasn't the name the man's parents gave him.

Two men held the horse while Gene threw on the saddle and cinched it down tight. He mounted, screwed himself down tight, and yelled, "Turn him loose!" The horse bellowed and pitched straight up and sideways in a frantic attempt to unseat the rider. It was an old story to Gene, but the big blue had a little more to offer than most horses. Gene wasn't afraid of riding the horse, but there was some doubt in his mind whether the horse could be broken. Since the first pitch, the animal had not lessened his fury and power. It looked like a long, rough ride.

Then something happened. Gene felt the saddle begin to shift under him. He gripped tighter with his knees, but with each frenzied pitch the saddle shifted further to the side. The cinch was giving, breaking. This had never happened before, and Gene had to decide instantly what was to be done. He decided to jump, realizing the horse was a potential killer if he caught him on the ground. On the other hand, if he stayed with the saddle, he would soon be caught beneath the horse and his thrashing hoofs. He jerked his boots clear of the stirrups, tossed the reins, and leaped clear of the raging hurricane deck. He bit the dust on his knees. The big horse turned instantly to trample his tormentor to bits, rearing into the air, his eyes fixed on his human tormentor. He paused for an instant, motionless in midair, slumped, then came crashing to the ground a few yards from where Gene lay. Gene saw a small hole above one of the horse's eyes from which a small trickle of blood seeped out. Someone had shot the horse, someone with sense enough to realize what was happening and with enough speed and accuracy to fire in time to save the rider's life.

Gene gathered himself up from the dust and looked around the corral. "Mr. Hawkins" was quietly slipping his smoking gun back into its holster. Gene went over to the dead horse, knelt down, and examined the saddle rigging: the hair cinch had been cut nearly through with a knife—an old enemy had performed the dirty work. Rhodes walked over to Hawkins, extended his hand, and said, "Thank you for saving my life. Which way are you riding?" The stranger smiled briefly and answered, "I'm going your way, since I have been your guest for the past two weeks in the back pasture."

"Hawkins" was invited to come to the ranch and go to work, but the stranger refused, saying he was Bill Doolin and a posse might show up anytime looking for him. Gene offered him a horse to replace the one that had been killed, but

Doolin refused. As he rode beside the quiet outlaw, Gene wondered why such a man should be wasted. With his level-headed courage and the intelligence he had already shown, it seemed a shame that the man should wind up as rifle fodder. When they reached the well, Doolin raised his hand in a farewell salute and rode north into the back hills. This was the last time Rhodes ever saw Doolin.

Doolin and West remained around their camp for a few days, then decided they had better get moving again. Doolin was eager to see his wife and son, and West wanted to see civilization again. Little Dick elected to stay in New Mexico and hire out as a cowhand, which he did until the summer of 1897, when he returned to Oklahoma Territory to help organize a new band known as the Jennings gang.

Bill Doolin drifted back across Texas and No Man's Land to Kansas, looking for a place to settle down and have his family join him. The final selection was Burden, a quiet little cattle town in eastern Cowley County at the edge of the Flint Hills where no one knew him. He got word to Edith to bring their team, wagon, household goods, and little Jay, and he would meet them along the way. Dr. Pickering reported that "Doolin disappeared and no one knows where. Also Edith Ellsworth. They probably went off together." This reflects the fact that few people were aware of Doolin's whereabouts or that he and Edith were married.

Edith and Jay joined Doolin in mid-May, 1895. They drove west from Burden a mile and a half, then camped near Silver Creek Ford not far from Uncle Johnnie Wilson's farm. Edith went to the Wilson farmhouse to buy milk, butter, and eggs.

In the course of the conversation, she mentioned that they were on their way east to visit relatives but because of her husband's sickness they would have to stay in the area for a while until his malaria and rheumatism became better so he would be able to travel. Mrs. Wilson was impressed by Edith's story, and after talking it over with her husband, they decided to let the Doolins move into an old farmhouse with a dirt floor located near their own house. The Wilsons furnished it with an old bed, two or three chairs, a table, and an old stove, and invited them to stay until Bill was able to travel. Mrs. Wilson drove into Burden the next day and called on Dr. Henry Manser to explain the Doolins' plight to him. As an act of charity, the doctor treated Doolin while the family was at Burden.

Winter came and Bill's health improved. He made frequent trips to Burden to buy coal, horse feed, and supplies. John Tedlie was the coal and feed merchant, and Doolin always sat in the seat of the wagon while Tedlie scooped coal into the wagon and loaded the feed. The stranger who said his name was Thomas Wilson always wore a long black overcoat and complained about his rheumatism. The long coat kept hidden the short Winchester saddle gun and the six-shooter Doolin always carried, just in case.

Here in Burden, Doolin knew the first peace he had had in years. Evenings he would sit near the old heating stove, his cane-bottomed chair tilted against the wall, and whittle with his worn bone handled barlow knife. He would watch Edith as she did the evening dishes and little Jay as he played with the old coffee grinder on the dirt floor. The old outlaw days seemed far away and gone forever.

It was while Bill was in one of these mellow moods, and in view of his health and family, that he decided to look up his old friend and employer Oscar Halsell and offer to give himself up, pay his debt to society, and live out his days with his family in peace. So, in late December, 1895, Doolin got in touch with Halsell and asked him to make arrangements with the federal officers, agreeing to give himself up, provided arrangements could be made whereby he could make restitution for his misdeeds by serving out a short term in the penitentiary. Marshal Nix would have none of it, contending that Doolin had killed three men, the marshal's own men. Three years of intensive search had been made for Doolin, and the federal government had spent $50,000 in the effort to apprehend him. Nix claimed he had spent more than $2,000 of his own money in addition to that spent by the government, so he would make no such deal with Doolin.

It had been said of Doolin that he "was probably the most killed" outlaw in the Territory. If no one was sure who a dead outlaw might be, the body was labeled as Doolin's until identification was absolute, for Doolin was worth $5,000 dead or alive. On August 8, 1895, the *Stillwater Gazette* had made the following observation: "The man recently killed by authorities near Hennessey has been identified as Bill Doolin. Poor Bill will be surprised to learn that he met such a tragic death while he knew nothing about it!"

Early in January, 1896, Doolin disappeared from Burden.

Edith and little Jay drove the team and wagon back to Lawson to her father's home. Doolin had heard of the healing powers of the baths at Eureka Springs, Arkansas, and when Nix turned down his proposition, he decided to go there for the cure.

In the meantime, Charlie Pierce and Bitter Creek Newcomb had drifted back to the Bee Dunn farm near Ingalls. On the night of May 1, 1895, they rode up to the farm, unsaddled their horses, ate supper, and went upstairs to bed, for they were very tired. The price on the head of each of these outlaws was now $5,000, dead or alive—the same as that against their leader, Doolin—and the Dunns wanted the money badly. That night, Bee Dunn and his brother John slipped out of their beds, got their guns, and cautiously went upstairs to the room where Newcomb and Pierce lay sleeping. At a signal, they opened fire on the sleeping pair and killed them both. Bee used Dr. W. R. Call's old eight-gauge shotgun, John a Winchester rifle. Bitter Creek was shot in the head and body, and Charlie Pierce hit by buckshot, also had wounds in the bottom of his feet, indicating that he was slain while lying down.

The Dunns hitched up a team, spread out a tarpaulin in the bottom of the wagon box, placed the bodies of the two outlaws on it, along with their guns, and covered them up. Then Dal and John started for Guthrie to claim the rewards. Bee remained at the ranch to clean up the mess in the upstairs "executioner's chamber" where the shooting had taken place.

Shortly before 2:00 P.M. on May 2, their wagon and jaded

team pulled up on the east side of the Capitol Hill water tower in Guthrie, and one of the Dunns got down and walked into town to report at the marshal's office while the other stood guard with his Winchester. The marshal's office dispatched a horse-drawn hearse from Spengle's Funeral Home to pick up the bodies. The rumor was soon afoot that dead outlaws were at Spengle's, and a large crowd gathered, demanding to see the bodies. The pressure became so great that the undertaker was forced to open the doors to the public, and for three hours a steady stream of curious people passed through the rooms to view the two bodies.

In the meantime, the dead men had been identified as Charlie Pierce and George Newcomb. Both men were dressed in blue overalls, calico shirts, and string ties. They wore regulation high-heeled boots with bronco spurs. Each man wore a well-filled cartridge belt. In Pierce's pockets were found a common pocket and dirk knife, a few coins, a rabbit's foot, and twenty-six Winchester cartridges.

Bitter Creek's pockets yielded a knife, a deck of cards, a small hand mirror, smoking tobacco, sixteen books of cigarette papers and twenty-four Colt .45 and Winchester cartridges. Their saddle bags were also examined and found to contain cartridges, tobacco, and other trail needs. Newcomb's saddle bags yielded up an empty Wells Fargo money bag and three pocket knives. Other possessions were two black Stetson hats, two Winchesters, and two Colt .45 revolvers.

On being stripped, Pierce's body was found to be literally riddled by buckshot fired at close range. Almost any one of the wounds would have proved fatal. All had entered the front of his body and ranged upward, the holes covering the body from the soles of his feet to the top of his head. His eyes were still open, and a sardonic grin was on his lips. The body was badly swollen, and he appeared to have been dead for some time.

Newcomb's body contained five bullet wounds: four in the head and one in the neck. One bullet had torn away a part of his forehead and exposed his brain; one of his arms was stiffened and raised as if to ward off a blow. He looked perfectly natural, as if he had not been dead very long.

The Dunns accounted for the differences in the appearance of the two bodies by saying they thought they were both dead when loaded into the wagon, but Bitter Creek was still alive and was revived by the jolting of the wagon. He pleaded with the Dunns to spare his life, but to no avail—they shot him again in the head, then proceeded on their journey to Guthrie. They were taking no chances on his talking and their losing the reward money.

Preparations were made by Marshal Nix to bury the two outlaws in the boot-hill section of Guthrie's Summit View Cemetery at government expense. On May 4, the parents of Bitter Creek Newcomb came to Guthrie and, after identifying their erring son, took charge of the remains. They buried Bitter Creek on their farm at Ten Mile Flat, located on the north bank of the Canadian River west of Norman, Oklahoma Territory. Charlie Pierce was buried in Summit View Cemetery on May 5 in "pauper's grave No. 65."

The capture and conviction of Arkansas Tom and the deaths of Tulsa Jack Blake, Bitter Creek Newcomb, and

Charlie Pierce were telling blows on Bill Doolin's gang. Four of his most faithful were in prison or dead at the hands of Marshal Nix and his men. Doolin had adequate warning that the end of the good old days was at hand.

And still another man was about to get his. Little Bill Raidler, Doolin's close lieutenant and long-time friend, was still on the conscience of Bill Tilghman. Bill had traced Little Bill into the Osage Nation, eighteen miles south of Elgin, Kansas. At the Moore Ranch, Bill learned that Raidler was hiding out in the timber by day and coming into the ranch headquarters for food at night. Tilghman hid out to watch and to wait. On the evening of September 6, shortly after sundown, Raidler came out of the timber and walked through the corral and past the well and chicken house. Tilghman waited until it would be impossible for him to miss Little Bill with his double-barreled shotgun. He then stepped out in the open and ordered Raidler to throw up his hands. At the sound of the familiar voice, Raidler drew his six-guns and got off one shot in Bill's direction. Tilghman fired, and the blast of buckshot at close range knocked Raidler off his feet. He was still alive when Tilghman reached him. He had six wounds: one in each side, two in the back of his head, one in his neck, and one through the right wrist. He begged to die rather than submit to capture. Tilghman got water and bandages and administered first aid, then put him in a wagon and drove him to a doctor at Elgin. Within a few days, Raidler was moved to the federal jail in Guthrie, where he slowly recovered from his wounds. Although he was in Guthrie, several other places bid for him in order that he might be tried for other crimes. The fifth regular member of the Doolin gang was out of circulation.

Unknown to Bill Doolin, Tilghman picked up his trail in Burden and followed him to Eureka Springs within ten days of his arrival there. Doolin had lived so long at Burden without being recognized or disturbed that he had grown a little careless. He felt that no one would be looking for him in a health resort, and the baths would be good for his rheumatism. He was well acquainted with Tilghman, but on the morning of January 15, 1896, when Tilghman walked through the bathhouse of the Davy Hotel where Doolin was sitting reading a paper, Doolin did not recognize him. The marshal was disguised in a Prince Albert coat, a black derby hat, and all the accessories. After Tilghman had passed on into the back room, Doolin continued reading his newspaper but had an uneasy feeling that he knew the man from somewhere.

The next thing Doolin knew, Tilghman stood four feet away with a .45 pointed at his heart, ordering him to put up his hands and surrender. Doolin got to his feet slowly, protesting his innocence, saying he had done nothing for which he would be wanted by the marshal. As he reached for his Colt in a shoulder holster—the same gun Deputy Marshal Lafe Shadley carried at Ingalls—Tilghman jerked his wrist and said: "Bill, don't make me kill you!" Realizing he would be killed if he resisted, Doolin raised his hands and surrendered. The hotel proprietor reluctantly took Doolin's gun on orders from Tilghman, then fled. Doolin was handcuffed, his gun was recovered, and he was taken to his hotel, where his belongings were picked up. Tilghman then went to the telegraph office and sent Marshal Nix the following telegram:

> Eureka Springs, Arkansas
> Jan. 15, 1896

U.S. Marshall Nix
Guthrie, Oklahoma Territory
  I have him. Will be home tomorrow.

> Tilghman

Doolin later said that if he had known Tilghman was alone, he would never have been taken.

After gathering up their belongings at the hotel, Tilghman, with Doolin in tow, went to the railroad station and caught the first train out. Tilghman kept Doolin's nickle-plated Colt as a trophy. Stowed away in Doolin's inside pocket, carefully wrapped and preserved in a sheet of note paper yellowed with age, creased, and almost worn through, Tilghman found a sheet of paper. On one side were some figures; on the other, written in a feminine hand, was sentiment in verse as follows:

> Good-bye
>
> How often by that lonely road
> Our pleasure has been riven.
> Good-bye is often said on earth
> But never said in heaven.
> Be ever true to your manhood
> That your life will be prosperous
> And a happy one and earnest
> Wishes of your friend.
> Learn to think for thoughts are noble
> Learn, oh learn to think aright

And everybody thoughts and actions
Then press on with all your might.
Live to make life grand and noble
Live to make it pure and true.
Learn to act your own part bravely,
Learn to think and learn to do.

The news of Doolin's capture swept the Territory like wildfire, and people flocked to Guthrie for a glimpse of the most infamous of all the Oklahoma outlaws. At Lowrie, a switch stop north of Guthrie, Deputy Ed Kelly got on the train as an extra guard. When the train whistled for the Cimarron River bridge, half the population of Guthrie was gathered at the station, on the platform and, on the tops of all the railroad cars near by. It was estimated that five thousand people waited for a look at the outlaw. Probably a thousand more waited for their chance to see him at the federal jail, where they knew the trail would end.

Marshal Nix, John Hale, and Deputy Heck Thomas met the train, the three officers, with Ed Kelly, falling in before and behind Tilghman and Doolin—and the crowd opened up to let them pass. When Doolin stepped down from the train, he carried a gold-headed walking cane like the one Bat Masterson made famous. He was wearing a narrow-brimmed hat and a store-bought suit, and his shackles clinked with each step. The "entourage" marched to a waiting cab and Doolin was loaded in, but not before the marshals had spent about twenty minutes having their pictures made while talking to newsmen. W. T. Ramsey, an old friend of Doolin, rode his horse up to the side of the cab to offer his gun to Doolin, but thought better of it, since he saw no way out of the crowd at that time. Heck Thomas rode shotgun with the cab driver on top while the other officers were jammed inside with Doolin for the ride to the marshal's office and the formal checking in at the jail.

It was a very festive occasion. Marshal Nix felt that the end of such a long search and the capture of the king of the Oklahoma Territory outlaws should have top billing, especially since so many people had come to Guthrie to see "the outlaw who couldn't be captured." The driver was ordered to make a tour of the city so all could see Doolin and the victorious marshals.

After leaving the station, Tilghman drove east up Oklahoma Avenue past the First and Last Chance Saloon and the Forman Saloon at 311 West Oklahoma Avenue, over which was located the Dixie Hotel, a cheap whorehouse with a cover charge of fifty cents. Each room was equipped with a girl, a bed, and slop jar. A pimp worked the street below to the corner of Oklahoma Avenue and Second Street. On the northeast corner was located the Commercial Bank Building, completed on October 1, 1889, the first brick and stone structure to be built in Oklahoma Territory. When the bank opened for business, the front of the building had not been finished, but there was a counter and an iron safe inside and everyone rushed in to put their money in the safe. Across the street south was the post office, on the government acre, and directly across the street west was the Acme Saloon. On the corner now occupied by City Hall was another saloon.

At this latter corner, the group turned south to pass the

most famous corner in the Territory for a number of years: at the intersection of Second and Harrison, on the northwest corner, was located the Reaves Brothers Casino, one of the most notorious gambling houses in the Southwest. The business had opened in a tent on April 23, 1889, the day after the opening, and soon after that there went up a frame building which was later replaced by one of brick. The owners claimed their doors were never closed, day or night, for fifteen years after the opening of the Territory. They advertised wines, liquors, and cigars, the most magnificent bar in the city, handsome billiard and pool parlors, gentlemen clerks in attendance, a barber shop, and large bathrooms. A sign with large black letters over the bar proclaimed:

> We the citizens of Guthrie are law-abiding people But to anyone coming here looking for trouble, we always keep it in stock with a written guarantee that we will give you a decent burial. We will wash your face, comb your hair and polish your boots. Place your sombrero on your grave and erect a memento as a warning to others saying he tried and failed.

On the northeast corner was located the Blue Bell Saloon, regarded as catering to the most genteel gentlemen with a thirst or a yen for gambling. It was here in 1903 that Tom Mix, the western movie star, tended bar for Jack Tearney and his high-class trade.

On the southeast corner of the intersection was the International Building, which housed several territorial legislative sessions upstairs. On the ground floor was one of the four locations of the Lillie Drugstore, and to the east was the Columbian Barber Shop, where E. W. Knowlton concocted his well-known product "Danderine." He absolutely guaranteed it to grow hair on bald heads and permanently cure all diseases of the scalp in every case. On the fourth and last corner, the southwest, were the Palace Hotel and the Palace Saloon. These four corners later became the favorite hangout of Will Rogers, Tom Mix, and Zack Mulhall.

The cab passed the Cammack Livery Barn—later known as Hoover Brothers—to Perkins Street and then turned east past the infamous White Elephant, operated by Stella Davenport but owned by an eastern syndicate. Here were the high-class and high-priced call girls. On north up Vine Street went the cab, passing the Green Tree, where all the girls were Creoles direct from New Orleans and not quite as expensive as Stella's beauties. From here the entourage went over to Broad Street and north to Harrison, then east past the Royal Hotel and Brook Opera House, where Lon Chaney of movie fame was later a stage hand at three dollars a week and slept on a property couch backstage. Many high-class attractions were booked here, including John Philip Sousa and the Marine Band, the St. Louis Symphony, and many of the top road shows of the day.

The cab finally pulled up in front of the Harriott Building, which housed the marshal's office and the territorial and federal courts. A large crowd had gathered, and it was a considerable time before Doolin and the marshals were able to make their way upstairs to Marshal Nix's office. Doolin was greeted by a large number of deputies and leading citizens. The press of the crowd became so great that the doors were opened and people were allowed to pass through and have a look at Doolin and Tilghman. Several thousand persons passed by in a steady stream for over an hour, and most of them shook hands with Doolin. One chunky little blonde remarked: "That's not him. I just know it isn't. He doesn't even look very bad. I could capture him myself." Doolin's answer was: "Yes, ma'am, I believe you could!"

Bill Doolin was quite the hero of the day. He told Marshal Nix that he had done no wrong except to get mixed up with bad company and to have the sins of others laid at his door. He told Nix he was glad the chase was over and he could have a fair trial and prove his innocence. He said he had wanted to give himself up but feared being killed for the reward money without being given a chance.

At 2:00 P.M., in the company of Deputy Tilghman, Marshal Nix, and a few other deputies, Doolin ate dinner at the Royal Hotel, the finest and most palatially important in the Territory, at the invitation of H. H. Perry, the proprietor. Half an hour after dinner, Doolin was escorted to the federal jail, located at the corner of Noble Avenue and Second Street. The jail had been constructed by a stock company of Guthrie men and then leased to the federal government. Later it was sold to the United States at a tremendous profit. Here most of the notorious outlaws of the early territorial days were imprisoned at one time or another. Today the remodeled building houses a Nazarene church.

The jail, built of native red sandstone, was about 45 by 100 feet in size, two stories high, with walls two feet thick. The only entrance to the main structure was a heavy steel door ten feet from the ground with a steel cage outside on the west wall. It was reached by an iron stairway enclosed on every side, with steel bars and a steel-barred gate at the foot. Every window was double barred, and the walls of several cells were reinforced with more steel. The flat roof had a three-foot stone wall, or rampart, all around.

Inside the front door of the jail, one was confronted with the stench of the place, one all its own, the odors of urine, tobacco, sweat, smoke, and stale cooking all blended. Beans, cabbage, and corn bread announced that this was a frontier jail. There was a large corridor, with a desk along the north wall, and a stairway, leading into the basement, located in the northwest corner. Here the guards were stationed.

The door to the bullpen was near the north wall on the east side of the guard room. Boxes with the combination control of the cell door also opened into the jailer's room. The bullpen occupied about half of the remainder of the upper floor. The rest of the space was taken up by a larger cell at the front of the bullpen and thirteen small cells located along the east wall and extending halfway west on the north and south walls. The kitchen, laundry, and several solitary cells were located in the basement. This completed the jail's pretentious offerings to its inmates.

By 3:30 P.M. on that day, the steel door of the federal jail clanged shut behind Doolin, and for the first and only time in his life he was behind bars. The most notorious of all western outlaws was at last a federal guest. It had taken more than eight years and had cost the federal government more than $50,000—not to mention the lives of several brave men—to put

Bill Doolin, "the king of the Oklahoma outlaws," behind bars.

When Doolin checked in at the federal jail, he discovered that his old partner, Bill Raidler, was already on the guest list, although pretty badly shot up. Doolin was also in bad health, and while in jail he was treated a number of times by Dr. Smith, the government physician for federal prisoners.

As soon as Edith Doolin received word at Lawson, Pawnee County, that Bill was in the Guthrie jail, she hitched up a horse to an open cart, dressed little two-year-old Jay for a cold ride, and started the long trip to Guthrie. She drove as far as Perkins on Monday, where she spent the night, and drove on to Guthrie the next day. Immediately on arriving, she went to the jail and was admitted to see her husband, the prize prisoner of the institution. The meeting was very affectionate, and little Jay wanted his father to go home with them. After a long conversation with Bill, Edith and Jay went to a boardinghouse, staying there for the next few days before going back to Lawson, where Edith was living with her parents.

Bill Tilghman received many congratulations for his capture of Doolin, and there was great speculation concerning the reward money he would receive. Most of it was conditional, however, on conviction after arrest, if alive, or was to be paid upon identification of the body in case the outlaw was delivered dead. Bill Doolin was not yet convicted, and he was very much alive. Wells, Fargo Express Company, however, paid Tilghman three hundred dollars at once, and this was all he ever received of the several thousand dollars that was supposed to be the reward.

On January 24, 1896, Marshal Nix was removed from office and Patrick S. (Pat) Nagle, a young lawyer from Kingfisher, appointed to replace him. To Nagle fell the task of keeping Doolin in jail and delivering him up for trial. On March 10, a guard discovered an underground tunnel that Doolin, Raidler, and Bob Montgomery, with the help of several others, had dug under the wall of the jail. Several knives and revolvers were taken from the 112 prisoners in the jail at the time. Doolin had made the statement that he would never wait for trial, but would escape or die in the attempt. Apparently he was making the attempt.

Bill Raidler was removed from the jail on April 10 and transferred to Kingfisher to stand trial for his part in the robbery of the mail train at Dover. On April 11, he was tried, found guilty, and sentenced to ten years in the federal prison at Columbus, Ohio. While serving his term, he developed locomotor ataxia as a result of his old wounds and was given a parole because of his illness. He returned to Oklahoma but never rode the outlaw trail again. He remained a cripple for the rest of his life and finally died as a result of his duel in the cattle corral with Bill Tilghman, who had received $1,800 in combined rewards for the capture and conviction of Raidler from the Rock Island Railroad, the Wells, Fargo Express Company, and the United States government.

On June 20, Deputy Marshal Frank Canton arrived at the federal jail with Dynamite Dick, whom he had picked up in Paris, Texas, where Dick was serving a thirty-day sentence for a liquor violation. When Doolin saw Dick, he was quite upset, for the marshals were fast rounding up his henchmen.

Doolin's trial was set for May 1 at Stillwater, where the indictment in Case No. 139 was for murder in connection with Bill's part in the Ingalls battle and in Case No. 140 for resisting arrest in the same place. When arraigned, Doolin made a deal with Hale, Tilghman, and the U.S. district attorney to plead guilty on the promise of a fifty-year sentence, which was the term received by Arkansas Tom for the same crimes at Ingalls. Tilghman and Reynolds took Doolin to Stillwater to face the murder charge on May 1. The judge asked how he would plead, and Doolin replied: "Not guilty." The judge then ordered him returned to the federal jail at Guthrie until further orders from the court.

A number of good men in the Territory would have been pleased to have seen Doolin stand trial and come clean—if it were possible for this to happen. Doolin also knew that in many cases it was hard to secure a conviction when a thief was tried by a cow-thief jury before a cow-thief judge.

Doolin proved to be a great celebrity at Stillwater, and crowds of people thronged the courtroom for a look at him. The two officers returned Doolin to jail on May 2 to await the next term of court. On the way back to Guthrie, Tilghman questioned Doolin about the reason he had changed his mind and pleaded not guilty, pointing out that he would hang if he ever went to trial. Doolin replied that fifty years was a mighty long time and he might beat the charges.

For a second time Guthrie's federal jail door clanged shut behind Doolin, and he settled down to scheme and wait. While he was in jail, a number of his friends and acquaintances visited him, among them Cliff McCubbin, Jim Williams, Dr. J. H. Pickering, and W. T. Ramsey of Cleveland, Oklahoma Territory. Doolin was not in the best of health, and the confinement, as well as his old wounds, was working against him. He lost weight and was put under the care of Dr. Smith. But Doolin had drive and a strong will, plus a desire to be free and join his family. Most of all, he hoped to bury the past forever.

9

AMBUSH AT LAWSON

DOOLIN, DYNAMITE DICK, and several others were cooking up a plan of escape. At nine o'clock each night, the prisoners were locked in their individual cells. On Sunday, July 5, 1896, at 8:45, a night guard, J. W. Miller, took off his gun and placed it in the box at the side of the front door. He took the cell keys and was admitted to the bullpen by the other night guard, J. T. Tull. Miller started toward the row of cells at the rear and along the east wall in the corner of the corridor to the right of the door, where the water bucket sat. This bucket of water was placed in such a manner that the prisoners could reach through the bars and get a drink when they wanted one. It was the custom of the inmates to fill tin cans with water and·take these to their cells just before lockup time.

The guard thought nothing amiss when he observed that George Lane, a huge half-Cherokee, half-Negro desperado with a long criminal record, was standing near the door. Lane's water can was too large to pass through the bars, so Miller asked Tull to help Lane get some water as he walked toward the rear cells. Tull unlocked the door and handed in the bucket of water for Lane to help himself. The brawny mixed blood pushed through the door with a lunge and grabbed Tull, pinning his arms to his sides in a bearlike hug. Three other prisoners—Walt McClain, Bill Jones, and Lee

Deputy U.S. Marshal William (Bill) Tilghman much as he looked the day he took Bill Doolin into custody at Eureka Springs, Arkansas.

Dave Fitzgerald's half-dugout at Pleasant Valley in Oklahoma Territory was a favorite hangout for Bill Doolin and the Daltons before the Coffeyville, Kansas, robbery.

Spearville, Kansas, about the time of the Doolin robbery in 1892. The Ford County Bank was located in the large brick building at the right.

Courtesy Kansas State Historical Society

A busy 1895 trade day in Clayton, Oklahoma Territory. Bill Doolin hid out here in the back room of C. A. Mackenzie's store on several occasions and ate many a good meal at Charley Burns's hotel.

The upstairs floor of this native red sandstone building at the corner of Division and Harrison avenues in Guthrie, Oklahoma Territory, housed the federal court and the U.S. marshal's office.

Rebuilt log house on the site of the Pierce Livery Stable at Ingalls, Oklahoma. Note the signs marking the old townsite and points of historical interest.

The third and last of the known Bill Doolin sidearms is this single-action Frontier Army Colt, .38 W.C.F., serial number 168010. Pictured with it are the Henry Starr holster and Jack Campbell's gunbelt.

Courtesy Shy Osborn

Pocket watch and match case taken from the body of Bill Doolin after the ambush at Lawson, Oklahoma Territory. Note the dent in the back of the watch case where it was hit by buckshot.

Killian—rushed in and knocked Tull to the floor. Killian grabbed the guard's revolver from its shoulder holster. At the same time, Lane picked up an iron bar and Jones armed himself with a hatchet lying on the table.

At the sound of the commotion, Miller turned and ran forward to help Tull, but before he had gone half a dozen steps, Doolin sprang through the open door and retrieved Miller's gun from the box. They dragged Tull to the center of the corridor in front of the steel cell door and ordered him to open the combination locks to Dynamite Dick's cell—or die. Killian held a revolver on the guard, as did Doolin, and Jones stood over him with a hatchet. Bill Dean, a trusty, was sitting at a desk in the corridor, and he ran to help Tull. Doolin knocked him down with the revolver, and the others dragged and kicked Dean to the stairway and down to the basement.

After the combination was worked and the cells opened, eight more prisoners, led by Dynamite Dick, joined the crowd. The prison break was well on its way. Killian and Jones took Tull's keys, went back to the bullpen, and invited the thirty-five inmates to join them. When all refused the invitation, Tull was locked in a cell. Before the prisoners left the jail, a fight broke out between two of them and Doolin covered the aggressor with the revolver and coolly informed him that another move of this kind would bring death.

With Doolin leading and Dynamite Dick close at his heels, the fourteen men marched out of the jail and down the steel stairs and disappeared into the darkness of the warm July night, each going his separate way. The prisoners who escaped included Bill Doolin; Walt McClain from Pawnee County, serving six months for larceny; Dynamite Dick; Lee Killian, also from Pawnee County, serving six months for whisky peddling; Bill Jones from Pottawatomie County, charged with counterfeiting; William Beck, charged with selling whisky in the Osage Nation; E. V. Hix, charged with perjury and held on bond forfeiture; Kid Phillips from Woods County, all-around tough outlaw, sentenced to one year for post-office robbery; Ed Lawrence from Kingfisher County, charged with post-office robbery; Bill Crittenden, serving one year from Pawnee County for larceny; Jim Block from Oklahoma County, under indictment for perjury; Charles Montgomery, serving ten months for larceny; and George Lane.

With the exception of Doolin and Dynamite Dick, only two of the escapees were ever captured or returned to jail. Beck came back on his own after the group separated north of town. Lawrence was later captured at his father's home near Enid by Deputy Marshal Smith. George Lane, the mixed blood, was arrested by Heck Thomas and Chris Madsen near Greenwood, a small town about thirty miles east of Kansas City, Missouri, after a brother in the Territory revealed his whereabouts.

Doolin and his three companions fled north on Second Street to the Santa Fe tracks and followed them out of town. After a half-mile run, Doolin's bad leg began to give him trouble, and he was forced to stop and rest. After a few minutes, they started on again. Beck elected to turn back to the jail and surrender. He gave himself up and reported the direction Doolin and his crowd had taken. Heck Thomas hastily organized a posse and gave chase.

The three remaining outlaws stayed together, but soon left the railroad tracks in favor of the dirt road that led north to Mulhall. About a mile from Guthrie, they heard a horse and buggy coming south on the road. They hurriedly hid themselves by the roadside, obscured by the darkness and tall weeds, and waited. Soon the buggy appeared. A clerk in the county treasurer's office, Alva W. Koontz, was driving Miss Winifred Warner, a schoolteacher, to Guthrie. As the buggy drew abreast of the jailbreakers, Doolin leaped onto the side of the buggy and the other two outlaws came up on the opposite side. Jones was still armed with the hatchet, and the young couple was quick to comply with Doolin's command as he poked his revolver into Koontz's ribs and ordered the two from the buggy. Doolin apologized, saying he was sorry to inconvenience them but it was necessary and he would return the buggy in the near future. The three fugitives climbed aboard and quickly disappeared into the night, still headed toward Mulhall.

Heck Thomas and his posse met the unfortunate couple at the edge of the city, hoofing it back to town. They gave Thomas an account of the holdup and described Doolin, Dynamite Dick, and the counterfeiter, Jones. The posse, now on a strong scent, set off at a grueling pace, but without success. Doolin had made good his first and only jailbreak. The posse returned to Guthrie, where they learned that the heat was on Marshal Nagle because of the jailbreak. He had made a standing offer of one hundred dollars for the capture of each of the ringleaders and twenty-five dollars for each of the other prisoners.

Deputies from the west headed for Stillwater and Ingalls. Those from the north converged on the Flat Iron country south and east of Pawnee. Posses from Guthrie combed the Cimarron bottoms from Cowboy Flats to Perkins and east to Ripley. It was the greatest manhunt in the history of the Territory. Nagle immediately put into the field thirty-two deputy marshals to hunt down and capture or kill the fugitives. People were demanding their capture—and soon—or they would be asking for a new marshal. The odds were sixteen to one in favor of the marshals, but for a long time even those odds were not enough to turn the trick.

Doolin and his two pals pushed north and east all night and hid out in the timber the next day. Jones decided to part company with Doolin and Dick and shift for himself. That night, Doolin and Dick hitched up the horse and headed for Morrison, sixteen miles east of Perry. Jones went west alone. On the night of the seventh, Doolin and Dick arrived at their destination, tied up the horse in the alley behind Grant Owen's saloon, and went inside. Bill Doolin held up the bartender with his stolen six-shooter, while Dynamite Dick gathered up some tobacco, whisky, and fifty dollars from behind the bar. Some objections were made by the bartender, and Bill Doolin promptly shot him through the ear. They made a hasty retreat and headed for the wild brakes along the Cimarron near Lawson, where Edith and Jay were staying with her parents.

The marshals strongly believed that Doolin had found a haven with friends in the Lawson area and was still in the county. Mrs. Doolin was closely watched, as were several places where Doolin was known to have hidden in the past. The fact was, he hid out in the back room of C. A. McKenzie's store at Clayton part of the time after he broke jail at Guthrie. After Doolin escaped, Marshal Nagle kept a number of his best deputies on Doolin's trail. Two of the last appointed for this task were Heck Thomas and Bill Tilghman.

Marshal Frank Canton of Pawnee also had some ideas about collecting the reward for Doolin's capture, so he made the trip out to Bee Dunn's farm and made a deal with Bee. If Bee would furnish information on Doolin—in case Doolin showed up in any of his old haunts or at the home of his father-in-law, Ellsworth, where Edith and Jay were still staying—he would share in the reward. In this way, he could be made a member of the posse that was to be formed.

Heck Thomas had the same idea, but he got to Bee later than Canton. Heck remembered the deal with the Dunns and the capture of Pierce and Newcomb. He was in a better bargaining position than Canton, however, for he was from Nagle's office, and there were some old charges, as well as some new suspicions, that could be pressed if desired. Bee agreed to supply any information he could get directly to Thomas in return for the promise that he was to be made a deputy and one of the posse members selected to make any capture. He was also to share in the reward money, and all the old charges would be dismissed. Thomas also commissioned Bee as a deputy U.S. marshal on the spot, as per his agreement with Nagle.

Heck also rode to Lawson and hired Tom and Charley Noble, blacksmiths who had a shop near Ellsworth's store and post office. They were to keep on the lookout for Doolin and report to Thomas the minute Doolin was seen in the area. Thomas was sure that, sooner or later, Doolin would come to see his wife and son. The Nobles were also promised a place in the posse and a share in the reward money. Tom Noble was staying at John Hoke's home, directly south and across the road from Ellsworth's, so he could lie in bed and watch for Doolin to make an appearance. Young Henry Hoke was Noble's apprentice in the blacksmith shop.

Doolin slipped in from his hiding place on the Cimarron River once or twice, but was unobserved. Finally, in a couple of weeks, Tom Noble saw him come in each night and leave early each morning, riding west. After making this observation several times, Tom decided to collect the reward money for himself and split it with no one.

Doolin usually came on horseback and nearly always left going west down the hill and across the Eagle Creek bridge. On several successive mornings, Tom slipped out of bed early and hid himself near the bridge and waited for Doolin to ride by. Noble would bring up his Winchester and take careful aim, but could not bring himself to pull the trigger, knowing full well he had only one shot and if he missed or only winged Doolin, he would surely be a dead man, for Doolin seldom missed. So each time he let Doolin pass, unaware of Tom's presence or intention. Tom didn't report his findings to Thomas at once because of his own plans; thus he prolonged Doolin's freedom a few weeks.

Doolin and Dynamite Dick had drifted to an old hideout on the north side of the Cimarron River on Mud Creek, twelve miles west of Ingalls. Here they were joined by Little Dick West. It was from this retreat that Doolin was making his trips to Lawson to see his wife and child—to plan his escape from the Territory. All the while, exposure to the elements, as well as his poor health, were working havoc with Doolin. He was losing weight and strength as time passed, and his bad leg became progressively worse. He felt that he would have to get away soon if he was ever to leave and go to a new place where he could rest and regain his health and strength. He planned to go to West Texas or New Mexico, where he was unknown, taking his family with him. With the help of his father-in-law, he had bought a wagon, a team, a plow, and a few household articles for the long journey. Tom Noble observed all these movements from the blacksmith shop and his own bedroom window. He approached John Hoke, asking him to help capture Doolin, but Hoke replied that he would have no part in killing the man. Hoke maintained it would be necessary to kill Doolin, for he would not be taken alive.

A day or so before August 25, Mack Hoke, younger brother of Henry, while playing in Tom Noble's upstairs room, found a heavy revolver under the pillow on the bed. He cocked the revolver, pointed it out the window, putting it near his cheek, took aim, and pulled the trigger. The not-too-well-held gun, too near the boy's face, recoiled savagely, and the hammer cut through his cheek. He let out a yell and dropped the gun to the floor. His mother came dashing up the stairs. Across the road, Edith Doolin heard the shot and also came on the run. She helped dress Mack's cheek wound. Edith was certain that the gun had been left there by Tom Noble, who never carried a revolver, but she did not mention this—or the fact that she knew Tom did not own a gun. She put two and two together and decided in her own mind that Tom was spying on her husband, perhaps with the thought of collecting the $5,000 reward.

When Bill came in that night, Edith called him aside and related the incident of Tom Noble's gun, cautioning him about a possible ambush. Bill remarked that there would be no one on the road, except possibly the Noble boys, and they were cowardly and he would scare hell out of them. He also told her he had a cart and horse hidden west of there and would ride over and pick up the outfit. She was to drive north and meet him at a location he indicated on a road that ran west and north.

During the night of August 24, Doolin rode up to the Ellsworth house and put his horse in the stable. No one knew when he came in, but he was there the next morning when the family got up. He kept out of sight all that day. After supper, Ira and Frank Ellsworth and Edith loaded Doolin's wagon. Just before dark, Doolin called Mrs. Ellsworth aside and told her he had prayed all day and had made up his mind that he was going to quit the outlaw business. He said that he, Edith, and Jay were leaving that night for West Texas or

New Mexico to make a new start. He also told her that if the marshals got him he would be trying to go straight, adding that he never knowingly killed anyone.

At Chandler, Heck Thomas received a telegram saying that Doolin and four others were in the Lawson area, that Doolin was seeing his wife, and that he was making plans to leave the country. Thomas had with him as deputies Rufus Cannon, a Cherokee-Negro mixed blood, who was one of his regular deputies, and his son, Albert. He set out at once for Bee Dunn's place east of Ingalls, where he picked up Hy Cotts (brother of Mrs. Bee Dunn), Dal, Bee, George, and John Dunn as posse members. They made a hurried ride to Lawson to meet the two Noble brothers. At Lawson, Heck got fresh news on Doolin and swore the Nobles into the posse. He posted his son, Albert, and Cannon on one road leading into Lawson, while George Dunn and Hy Cotts were assigned to another road. Thomas took with him the remainder of the posse, feeling certain that Doolin would surely leave by the west road, which he generally used.

Thomas stationed his remaining men in Hoke's cane patch west of the house and below the rock outcropping on the south, or Payne County, side of the road west of Ellsworth's house and a little east of Eagle Creek. Near the Eagle Creek bridge, it was the same spot Tom Noble had selected for his singlehanded capture of Doolin before he lost his nerve. The two Nobles, Tom and Charles, were hidden first. Next to them down the hill west were the three Dunns. Bill and Bee were armed with shotguns; all other members of the posse carried Winchesters. Bee had Dr. Call's old eight-gauge shotgun, loaded with buckshot. It was the same gun (belonging to his stepfather) he had used to kill Pierce. Thomas stationed himself in the final position on the far west end of the line next to Bee.

The posse settled down, prepared for a long wait. Heck kept a close watch on the house with the field glasses he had captured from outlaw Bill Cook in the Creek Nation some time earlier. There was much activity around the house as a wagon was loaded with the meager belongings of Doolin and his family.

After sundown—between eight and nine o'clock—Doolin went to the barn and saddled his horse, bade his wife good-bye, and started down the road west. He stalked slowly along the dark road from the house, his .40-.82 Winchester saddle gun cradled in the hollow of his left arm, his thumb on the hammer and his finger on the trigger as he tightly gripped the smooth walnut stock. He held the ends of the reins in his left hand, leading his fine saddle horse as he stepped forward, peering into the deep shadows along the road.

When he drew abreast of the cane field on the south side of the road, Heck Thomas suddenly shouted, "Halt, Bill!" Quick as a striking rattler, Doolin fired at the voice in the darkness, narrowly missing Thomas and Bee Dunn. He almost never missed, they knew. At that same instant, Bee Dunn, standing close to the right of Thomas, let go with Dr. Call's shotgun. Later Bee claimed the gun went off accidentally as he fired at the same instant Thomas told Doolin to stop. The second shotgun, in the hands of Bill Dunn, along with several rifles, cracked only seconds later, including

Heck's Winchester, which, by a strange coincidence, was also a caliber .40-.82. Heck fired twice. All of the shots went wild except the shotgun blasts of Bee and Bill Dunn, and one slug from Heck's rifle which caught Doolin in the right side. In the excitement, many rounds were pumped through the rifles without being fired. Tom Noble later told Henry Hoke, his apprentice, that he never fired a shot—he was so scared that he pumped his unfired cartridges out upon the ground.

Doolin lost his rifle as the double charge of buckshot struck him full in the chest, but he was still able to draw his six-gun and fire one shot, which went wild as he fell. It was the buckshot that did the job and put an end to Bill Doolin. He stretched out in the dust of the road on the Payne County side, twitched convulsively once or twice, and lay still, dead in a spreading pool of blood. The posse was a little reluctant to approach the body for fear Doolin might not be dead after all and might shoot one of them in revenge. But Oklahoma Territory's noted outlaw, a man who was known by his wife and small son as a devoted husband and father, by his friends as a man you could always count on, and by bankers, express companies, railroads, stockmen, and marshals by the nickname said to have been given him by Bill Tilghman, "the king of the Oklahoma outlaws," was dead.

Edith Doolin heard the shots, rushed from the house, and ran wildly down the road toward her slain husband. As she ran, she screamed, "Oh, my God! They've killed Bill!" Heck Thomas restrained her and would not let her near the body. She asked for it, but her request was refused. The marshals wanted the body—they had to have it—in order to collect the

$5,000 reward. Heck Thomas explained to her that they would deliver the body to the marshal's office in Guthrie and she would have to go there to claim it. He sent her back to the house.

It was agreed among the posse members that Heck Thomas would take the official credit for bringing in Bill Doolin, since they felt it would be much easier for him to collect the reward money than any of the others. He was to divide the money with them.

Thomas sent Tom and Charley Noble up the road to John Hoke's place with orders to rent a team and wagon from the farmer or, if necessary, to confiscate it. Tom told Hoke what Thomas wanted, and Hoke replied that his wagon was loaded with pole wood and the wagon box was off. The Noble brothers agreed to unload the wood and put the box back on the wagon. Hoke made it plain to Tom Noble that he would hold him personally responsible for the team and wagon while the rig was away from the farm.

The wood was quickly unloaded, the team of mules hitched up, some straw placed in the wagon box, and an old wagon sheet thrown on top. They drove down to the place where Doolin lay. Hoke followed the wagon down the hill, and when he came up to Doolin's body, he leaned over and felt of him. Still warm, Doolin lay on his back, gazing up at the stars with open, unseeing eyes.

Four of the possemen picked up Doolin's body and loaded it into the wagon, much as one would a dead hog, and covered it with the wagon sheet. Thomas picked up Doolin's .38 Colt and Winchester from the road and placed them beside the body in the wagon, along with Doolin's saddle. Thomas mounted the seat beside Tom Noble, and they set out for Guthrie. They were careful not to drive through Ingalls, since it was felt that Doolin had too many friends there who would not appreciate this grim deed.

As soon as Edith reached the house, she told her father what had happened, and Rev. Ellsworth directed his two sons, Frank and Ira, aged twelve and thirteen, respectively, to unload the wagon so Edith could make the trip to Guthrie at once. This was done, and not too long after the marshals had left, she was following them, accompanied by her two brothers and Jay.

The marshal's wagon made its weary way south and west. Before it reached Clayton, east of Perkins, Mrs. Doolin caught up with it and followed along behind. Shortly after dawn, they pulled into Clayton. Mrs. Doolin drove with little Jay asleep in her arms and her old sunbonnet pulled down over her drawn face. They all stopped at Charley Burns's hotel in Clayton for breakfast before proceeding to Perkins, across the Cimarron to Goodnight, and then west to Guthrie.

At 1:00 P.M., Heck Thomas and Tom Noble drove down Oklahoma Avenue and stopped the wagon, with its gruesome cargo, in front of a frame building (106 East Oklahoma) occupied by the Rhodes furniture and undertaking establishment. Heck stepped down and entered the building, where he was greeted by Neal Higgins, the undertaker in charge, who was alone at the time. Heck informed him there was a body for him out in the wagon, and Higgins directed Noble around to the alley in the rear of the building to the back door. Here the body was removed to the back room and placed upon a common table where all of the undertaking work was to be performed. Higgins immediately recognized the body as being that of Bill Doolin, whom he had seen on many occasions in Guthrie.

Dr. Smith, the government physician, was called in to make an examination, identification, and report on the body for the purpose of obtaining the reward money. Dr. Smith had attended Doolin during his six months in the federal jail and knew him quite well.

The wagon and team of mules, followed by old Shep, the dog, was driven over to Heck Thomas' house at 909 East Springer (the home is still standing) and the team unhitched. One mule was tied to each rear wheel of the wagon and the harness stripped from the mules. In a short time, Maggie Murphy, a little Irish woman who worked for Mrs. Thomas, came into the house and told her to have the men take the mules away from the wagon because the straw in the bottom of the wagon was covered with Doolin's blood and the mules were eating the straw. The straw was removed at once and burned, then the blood was washed out of the wagon box. In the meantime, word had leaked out that Doolin's body was at the Rhodes place, and a large crowd was gathering in the street to view the remains of the most noted outlaw in America.

Dr. Smith noticed that Doolin had on the same clothes he had worn in the federal jail and that during the past six weeks Doolin had lost much weight and had allowed his auburn hair and beard to grow. After the body had been stripped and washed, Doctor Smith made a postmortem examination and discovered twenty-one wounds, all above the waist, twenty resulting from the shotgun pellets, and one from a rifle ball. He also examined the head and removed the bullet lodged there during the Southwest City, Missouri, bank robbery. The ball had been carried in Doolin's brain for more than two years.

By this time, the crowd in the street had swelled to more than one hundred persons, each clamoring to be allowed to come into the building. Finally, they were allowed inside the store, but it was soon evident that the new furniture would all be ruined as people began to climb onto the tables and chairs to look over the heads of others for a glimpse of the stripped-to-the-waist dead outlaw. Doolin's body was then moved to a vacant portion of the Gray Building on South Division (where the telephone office was lately located) and put on public exhibition in the front window before being dressed and placed in a casket.

Neal Higgins was kept busy for the next few days by the hundreds who filed by for one last look at Bill Doolin. No less than two thousand people stopped to view the remains. Not everyone who came to see the body did so out of curiosity. Edith and Jay were there, as well as many friends and neighbors from Ingalls and Lawson. A widow's box was placed on the coffin into which small coins were placed for the relief of the widow and her child.

One man who viewed the body remarked that it looked to him as if Doolin had died and the marshal had filled his body with buckshot so that he and his posse might collect the

$5,000 "dead or alive" reward. This story reached the ears of a man named Hicks, who lived near Jennings and disliked Heck Thomas because Heck had sent him to jail for petit larceny. Hicks repeated the tale many times in order to discredit Thomas and embarrass the marshal's office.

Edith Doolin wanted a picture of her dead husband. Bruce Daugherty, a photographer, was called in and two pictures were made, one with the body propped up on a slab and bare to the waist, the second after the body had been dressed and placed in a casket. Copies of these two photographs were sold for twenty-five cents each, and prints can still be found in and about Guthrie. The cost of the casket was twenty-five dollars, and the total cost of embalming the body was fifty dollars, both fees being paid by the U.S. government.

10

THE END OF THE TRAIL

AN INQUEST WAS HELD on August 27, 1896, and the results were as follows:

In the matter of the United States vs. William Doolin charged with resisting arrest, a warrant was issued by Commissioner Buckner to the U.S. Marshal for service and was placed in the hands of Deputy Heck Thomas. The warrant was returned on the 25th of August, 1896, showing service upon the within named William Doolin at or near the Creek County line, and that in the service, while resisting arrest, the defendant, William Doolin, was killed. The body is produced in court.

B. J. Conley, being called and sworn upon oath, says:

Question: What official position, if any, do you hold?

Answer: Federal jailer at Guthrie, Oklahoma Territory.

Question: Are you acquainted with William Doolin?

Answer: Yes, sir.

Question: You may state whether or not he was ever in your custody.

Answer: He was.

Question: How and under what circumstances did he escape?

Answer: He broke jail on the night of July 5th.

Question: Of this year?

Answer: Of this year, yes sir, 1896.

Question: Have you examined the body produced by Deputy Thomas upon this warrant?

Answer: Yes sir.

Question: You may state whether or not that body is the remains of William Doolin.

Answer: It is.

Question: You may state if you know upon what charges he was committed at the time of his escape from the Federal jail here.

Answer: The charge was murder of an United States officer.

Mr. Thomas Phillips, being called upon his oath, says:

Question: What official position do you occupy?

Answer: Chief clerk of the Marshal's office at Guthrie, Oklahoma Territory.

Question: Do you know the person named in the within warrant, William Doolin?

Answer: Yes sir.

Question: Have you examined the remains?

Answer: I took charge of the body when it was brought in.

Question: Did you have an examination?

Answer: I did examine him.

Question: Are you able to identify these remains?

Answer: I am most fully.

Question: Of what person are they the remains?

Answer: William Doolin.

Question: Is that the Doolin who broke out of jail here when committed on the charge of murder of an United States officer and the Doolin mentioned in this warrant?

Answer: I do recognize him as such.

Question: You may state any additional marks giving the

description forwarded to your office for his identification in case of arrest.

Answer: We were informed that a bullet had lodged in his head during the fight over at a Southwest City, Missouri, bank robbery some years ago. After the body was brought in I made the examination for this mark and found there was a bullet embedded in his skull which had lodged there. I told Dr. Smith to make an operation and watched him perform the same during which he removed the bullet in the skull at the above location.

William D. Dunn, being called and sworn:

Question: Were you acquainted with William Doolin in his lifetime?

Answer: Yes sir.

Question: How long have you known him?

Anwer: I have known him about eight years, if not more.

Question: Have you examined the remains produced by Deputy Heck Thomas upon this warrant?

Answer: Yes sir.

Question: Do you know whose remains these are?

Answer: They are William Doolin's.

Question: Is that the Bill Doolin who was in the Federal jail here upon a charge of murder of an United States officer and who escaped from the jail in July?

Answer: Yes sir, it is.

Question: Did you ever have a conversation with William Doolin in which he told you he was in the Southwest City, Missouri robbery and at which time he was suffering from a wound in the head which he had received at the robbery?

Answer: Yes sir; I saw him sometime after, I don't know how long; it may be a week or ten days.

Question: State his condition at that time.

Answer: Yes sir seemed like it struck the front of the temple at about the edge of the hair and then glanced up and lodged over his eye. He said he received it in the fight at the bank robbery at Southwest City.

Question: Do you know of Doolin getting wounded in any other robberies from any statements he made to you?

Answer: Yes sir, I do.

Question: State when and where you met him and what he said.

Answer: He came to my place about a month after the robbery at Cimarron, Kans. I was talking to him about the wound he had in his heel, he was crippled then, he was walking with a crutch. Most of the time, he used his Winchester for a crutch. I ask him how he got shot. He said that he got into a fight in Western Kansas when he was coming east to rob a train, after he had robbed the train at Cimarron, Kan. He said that he did not know whether Marshals or sheriffs were after him who did the shooting but it was some parties who were after him for the robbery.

Question: Did you examine the wound at that time?

Answer: Yes sir, I dressed it for him several times.

Question: State the character of the wound.

Answer: It was shot right in the back of the heel up towards the ankle and top part of the foot at the side on the inside.

Question: Did he state to you what was done at the time of the robbery of the train at Cimarron, Kansas?

Answer: Yes sir, he did.

Question: What did he tell you?

Answer: Told me he held up the train that several shots were fired and during the fight they killed an express messenger.

Said they got a great deal of silver. Most of the money was silver. All the boys had their saddle pockets partly filled with silver when they came to my place. When the boys came in, Doolin was the only one that got touched in the fight.

Question: This person that you describe who said he received the wound in the head at Southwest City, Missouri, bank robbery who said to you that he was wounded in the heel during the fight at Cimmaron, Kansas, train robbery, is that the same Doolin who escaped from the Federal jail here and whose body is now produced in court upon the warrant, is he?

Answer: Yes sir.

U.S. of America
Territory of Oklahoma
County of Logan

I, W. W. Thomas a U.S. Commissioner of the First Judicial District of Oklahoma Territory, do hereby certify that the within embodies testimony submitted before me on August 27, 1896, at my office in Guthrie, Oklahoma Territory, and all the testimony submitted on said date.

W. W. Thomas

The marshal's office first thought it would be necessary to ship Doolin's body to Fort Smith, Arkansas, in order to collect the reward money. On the evening of August 27, the Wells, Fargo Express Company wired that it would not be necessary to ship the body. All that was required was positive identification.

Doolin's body remained at the Rhodes undertaking rooms until the night of August 27. Marshal Nagle sent word to Higgins that he was through with Bill Doolin's body and for him to bury it as soon as possible. The marshal's office ordered the grave dug that night. Neal Higgins went at once to 921 West University Street and got Sherman Patton, the cemetery sexton, out of bed to dig the grave. Patton didn't want to dig it at that hour of the night, but upon being offered five dollars extra, he was induced to do so at once.

He dressed, harnessed his horse, got his gun, and set out for the cemetery, which was north of town. Just before he reached the cemetery gate, his horse stopped with a snort. The animal lifted its ears and looked down the road ahead of them. Something white was moving around, and it looked as big as a house. One sexton was very scared. Then the thing moved—it was a cow. Same sexton very much relieved. The grave was completed before daybreak.

At eight o'clock on the morning of August 28, Bill Doolin was laid to rest by Neal Higgins and Sherman Patton, the Negro sexton of Summit View Cemetery, Guthrie, Oklahoma Territory. Doolin had joined his old saddle pal Charlie Pierce, who was buried near the new grave. Little Dick West was to join them later in a grave close by.

The only witnesses to the burial were Mrs. Doolin, two deputy marshals from Nagle's office, a man by the name of Sam Trimble, and a handful of curious townspeople. As the first clods of dirt sounded on the lowered casket, Mrs. Doolin sighed heavily and cried out: "Poor Bill, why did they kill him?"

After the people had gone and the grave was filled, Higgins instructed Patton to place an old buggy axle, which he had brought along for the purpose, at the head of the grave to mark the spot. This rusty, bent, and twisted axle marked Doolin's grave for the next sixty-three years, until a more appropriate marker was erected in 1959.

John Matthews, who married one of Mrs. Doolin's sisters, was first credited with the tipoff that resulted in Doolin's death. However, it was finally revealed by Thomas that Tom Noble supplied the information and that Matthews had nothing to do with the matter.

The $5,000 reward for the capture of Bill Doolin, dead or alive, was never paid in full. Heck Thomas received the following monies on Doolin:

U.S. jailer	$ 25.00
Wells, Fargo Express Company	500.00
U.S. government	250.00
People of Southwest City, Missouri	160.00
Missouri State Legislature	500.00
	$1,435.00

Heck paid out the following amounts:

Charley Noble	$ 36.00
Tom Noble	36.00
Bee Dunn	36.00
Dal Dunn	36.00
George Dunn	11.00
Heck Thomas	36.00
Rufus Cannon	10.00
Pearl-handled pistol purchased at Union City	25.00
Copies of evidence paid two stenographers	10.00
Trips to Southwest City, Sulphur Springs, Fort Smith, and return to Guthrie	42.00
Time lost on 3 trips, 7 days $5 per day	35.00

Cash paid photographer	15.00
Brought forward:	
Made two more trips to Southwest City out $50.00 and five days time about $100— charged	$35.00
Second trip to Fort Smith and return	22.00
Time lost, 5 days	25.00
Trip to Neosho, Mo. to check on reward	20.00
Trip to Jefferson City	25.00
Two round trips to Topeka, Kansas	30.00
Several other items for which no charge was made	
	$1,016.00

Heck divided the reward money among the men but Dal Dunn was dissatisfied, so Heck paid him money out of his own share. Cannon was a regular posse member and thus not eligible to reward, but Heck gave him some of his own share. When the division had been completed, Heck was out of pocket. Possemen shared any rewards collected unless they were paid as regular peace officers, in which case they received no part of the reward. The reward money in such cases was usually divided equally among the members of the posse, and this was one of the reasons the marshals often did not look with favor on posses. If a posse was needed, the marshals generally kept it small in numbers.

In the beginning of law in the West, rewards were usually posted for the capture of wanted men alive, upon conviction for their crimes. But too often an officer risked his life to capture a killer or robber and then the jury would set his prisoner free, which meant no reward for the officer. Finally, the only way an officer would go after an outlaw with a price on his head was to bring him in dead or alive. Some officers never brought in a live outlaw: dead men were never acquitted, and identification was all that was required in order to claim the reward.

After her husband's body had been laid to rest, Edith Doolin reported to Marshal Nagle's office to claim her husband's meager belongings, consisting of a fine saddle, his Colt revolver and Winchester rifle, a diamond ring found on his finger, a large Elgin watch, a match case, and several rounds of ammunition. The watch had a large dent in the back where one of the buckshot had struck it. The marshal refused to give up any of the articles except the watch, match case and ammunition, saying the officers thought the other items had been stolen.

Doolin had for years carried the watch, which he acquired in Arkansas City in the 1880s, and it was finally given to his son, Jay, who still has it in his possession or has passed it on to his heirs. Jay, as a doughboy in France, carried the watch all through World War I. Edith Doolin filed a $50,000 damage suit against the marshals for killing her husband, but it was finally dismissed at her request. On February 14, 1897, Mrs. Edith Doolin and Colonel Samuel M. Meek were married by James P. Long, a justice of the peace in Clarkson, Payne County, Oklahoma Territory.

Meek was an original Oklahoma Boomer and had homesteaded on a farm in Payne County. He had served with the Union Army during the Civil War. He was considerably older than his bride—he had a son about her age. They lived in Ingalls, where young Jay first attended school. In 1901, they moved to Kaw City, south of Arkansas City, Kansas, and in 1902 they moved again, this time to Beaver County, using Bill Doolin's team and wagon in making the move. While they were living in Beaver County, World War I came along and Jay enlisted and went to France. He returned unharmed and lived with the family until 1921. Colonel Meek died on July 2, 1917, and is buried in Clearlake Cemetery in Beaver County.

In 1921, Jay and his mother moved to Ponca City, where he found a job with the Continental Oil Company as a still man. He worked at this until his retirement at the age of sixty-five. He was never in any kind of trouble at any time, nor was any of his five children. Jay still lives at Ponca City.

For more than sixty-five years, the true identity of Jay Doolin was concealed from the general public because he took the name of his stepfather, which he still uses (he is known as Jay D. Meek). Mrs. Edith (Doolin) Meek died in 1928 at Ponca City and is buried in the I.O.O.F. Cemetery there.

In conclusion, several other incidents should be of interest, although they occurred after Bill Doolin's death. Bee Dunn's number was also about to come up, for he and Marshal Canton were now bitter enemies and Canton was pressing old charges in Pawnee County against Bee. This made Dunn very angry, and Canton, in turn, was at odds with Dunn because Dunn had given the information of Doolin's whereabouts to Thomas instead of to him as per the agreement the two had made. Their feud finally came to a head in Pawnee on the afternoon of Friday, November 6, 1896. Dunn was standing in front of the butcher shop on Main Street on the south side of courthouse when Canton passed him. Dunn stopped Canton and remarked: "Canton, I understand you have it in for me, by God." With these words, Dunn went for his gun, but Canton was too fast for him and shot Dunn, whose gun had stuck momentarily in its holster. Canton fired one shot and killed Dunn instantly. Dunn lay for some time in the street, with blood oozing from his mouth and a dark bullet wound in his head. Canton gave himself up to Sheriff Lake, but he was simply placed under guard. Dunn had been the shotgun trigger man in the killing of Bitter Creek and Doolin, but now he had received his own dose of hot lead. Canton regarded Bee Dunn as one of the fastest men with a gun he had ever known, and he felt that if Dunn had not had trouble with his holster, the shootout might have had a different ending.

When the Dunn brothers went to claim Bee's body, they threatened to burn the town and kill Canton. Saturday afternoon the family arrived in Ingalls with the body. They took Bee to his stepfather's home and kept the body until Sunday afternoon, then buried it in the cemetery at Ingalls, a long funeral procession following the hearse. Many of the people of Ingalls objected to Bee Dunn's being buried in their cemetery, but the family put him there anyway. The next morning, there was a pile of fresh hog entrails on the new grave—a protest by some of the dissatisfied. The Dunn family erected the largest and most impressive monument in the cemetery over Bee's grave. It is still standing and in good repair in the center of the Ingalls cemetery and may be viewed if you happen to pass that way.

The court found no bill against Canton for the killing of Bee Dunn and turned him loose at once. The public sentiment in Pawnee was for Canton because Dunn's reputation was against him. At Ingalls, the people were divided in sentiment on the case. All were expecting Dunn to be killed, but thought the job would be done by one of the remaining outlaws in revenge for Bee's part in the shotgunning of two of their members. Many of the townspeople felt that there would be more killings, either the Dunns or someone would get Canton. But this was the end of the Canton-Dunn feud, for Dal, John, and George skipped out: there were many bills against them in Pawnee for cattle stealing.

Three of Doolin's handguns were preserved for at least a time. It is strange that two of the guns passed through the hands of Bill Tilghman. The first Doolin gun was the one Bill traded to George Ransom, the saloonkeeper at Ingalls, for Deputy U.S. Marshal Lafe Shadley's gun, a single-action Frontier Army Colt, caliber unknown. Ransom kept the gun around the saloon for a time, but finally took it out to his farm, where it hung on a nail in the bunkhouse. The weapon finally disappeared from its place on the wall and was never recovered.

The second of Doolin's guns was the one carried by Marshal Lafe Shadley the day of the Ingalls shootout, September 1, 1893. As already noted, it was picked up by Mrs. Ransom at the corner of her house where the wounded Shadley had dropped it. She, in turn, gave it to her daughter, Mrs. Williams, who took it home with her to the farm west of town.

George Ransom later picked it up and took it to his saloon. Here Doolin saw it and, admiring it for its beauty and craftsmanship, traded the gun he was carrying for the Shadley weapon and paid a cash boot. This gun, too, was a single-action Frontier Army Colt, .45 caliber, serial no. 97445, nickle-plated, and fitted with ivory handles. Bill Tilghman took it from Doolin when he arrested him at Eureka Springs, Arkansas, in January, 1896, and added the weapon to his private collection.

Mrs. Zoe Tilghman stated that:

> Two or three years before his death in 1924, Tilghman exhibited the gun, along with several others, in the window of an Oklahoma City jewelry store, but during the night thieves smashed the plate-glass window and made off with three of the guns, the Doolin gun being one of them. They were never recovered. Bill Tilghman always thought Mexicans took the gun, probably unaware of its history.

New information reveals a gun in the Museum of the Great Plains in Lawton, Oklahoma, reputed to be the Shadley gun. This gun is definitely a fake. So Lafe Shadley's old Colt remains to be found by some lucky collector. New evidence also points to the fact that the gun was never stolen from the display window but was taken from the home by Woodie Tilghman, pawned, and never redeemed.

The third of Doolin's guns is another single-action Frontier Army Colt, .38 W.C.F., with a 4¾-inch barrel. Ten notches are cut in the right hand grip and the initials "JC" stamped on the right side of the frame just above the base of the trigger and guard. The serial number is 168010. This Colt was picked up by Heck Thomas after the ambush at Lawson, Oklahoma Territory, on the night of August 25, 1896. Doolin had fired the gun once and dropped it when he was mowed down by the shotgun blasts of the Dunn brothers, Bee and Bill. Heck later gave the gun to Bill Tilghman for his collection as a memento, since Tilghman had been so closely connected with the Doolin case for so many years.

Doolin had acquired the gun sometime between July 5, 1896, when he made his jailbreak at Guthrie, and August 25 of the same year. Where or from whom he got the gun is unknown, unless it was the one he took from the jail guard during his escape. If it was indeed the weapon the guard carried, it was also the one with which Doolin shot off the ear of the saloonkeeper, Grant Owen, at Morrison the night of the escape. The Colt was manufactured in 1896, as is revealed by the serial number. The gun was therefore very new at the time of Doolin's death.

Tilghman finally gave the gun to a friend, a young deputy named Jack Campbell. It was Campbell who stamped the initials "JC" on the right side of the frame. As a peace officer, Campbell carried the outlaw gun, now gone respectable, for the next fifty years. During this time, he served ably as a deputy under many sheriffs. To mention a few: Roy B. Church, W. R. Cody, Harry Cochran, W. A. Latimer, L. C. Geiger, Dick Johnson, C. E. Wright, Alvie Allison, and a number of others in Kansas, Oklahoma, and Texas.

No claim is made regarding the ten very old notches cut in the right hand grip, but they must have been carved there sometime after Doolin owned the gun, for he had it less than two months. During this period there is no record of his having shot anyone (with the exception of the saloonkeeper at Morrison, and he shot him only in the ear), much less ten men. If in fact he did cut the ten notches, it must have been for a pastime while he was hiding from the law.

Finally, in April, 1954, the .38 Colt of Bill Doolin, the Henry Starr holster, and the gunbelt, which was Jack Campbell's personal belt, were acquired by Shy Osborn of Clyde, Texas. The three items are now a part of his private collection and have an honored resting place on the wall of his den.

The .40-.82 Winchester carried by Doolin on the night of his death has never been satisfactorily accounted for—unless perhaps it is the one in my possession, serial number 37193. At one time, Jay Doolin Meek had some of the .40-.82 cartridges from his father's gun.

During the 1930s, Al Jennings, the reformed Oklahoma outlaw who became an evangelist, was in Guthrie for a preaching engagement and visited Doolin's grave in the company of City Manager John Hamill, and the Reverend L. L. Scott. They discussed putting up a permanent marker on Doolin's grave, but nothing came of the suggestion at that time. In April, 1960, however, an appropriate marker was placed at the head of Doolin's grave and the old buggy axle removed. I now have the axle as a memento of Oklahoma's turbulent past.

A large number of people interested in preserving historical points of interest in Oklahoma (Preston Walker, one-time mayor of Guthrie; the Payne County Historical Society; the Ingalls Activity Club; and many private individuals, including me—I headed the drive) contributed appreciable funds to erect a historical marker concerning Doolin. It is made of native Oklahoma pink granite and bears the inscription "William 'Bill' Doolin, 1858–1896." At the bottom of the marker are these words: "Killed August 25, 1896, near Lawson, Oklahoma Territory, by Deputy U.S. Marshal Heck Thomas and Posse." The marker can be found in the northeast section of Guthrie's Summit View Cemetery, just northeast of the toolhouse and on the east side of the draw that runs off in a northerly direction from the toolhouse.

In 1914, E. D. Nix, Bill Tilghman, and Chris Madsen formed the Eagle Film Company and produced a motion picture entitled *The Passing of the Oklahoma Outlaws*. Bill Doolin (that is, the man who played Bill Doolin) had a leading role, and Arkansas Tom, who had been pardoned from prison, played himself. The picture was quite a success and was shown all over the Southwest. Tilghman usually narrated the film (that was long before "talkies").

Walter (Spunky) Taylor, the last of Judge Park's deputies to die (December 15, 1961), credited Bill Doolin with saving his life. He said Doolin prevented another desperado from shooting him through the back one day. It wasn't "a fitting way for a good lawman to die," was Doolin's explanation for his interference in this possible killing.

Of the twenty-odd men who rode with Doolin at one time or another, all with one or two exceptions, died of gunshot wounds with their boots on. In fact, bullets ended the lives of most of the outlaws of the Old West. Most of them were physically tough, fearproof, had iron nerves, no conscience, were long riders who could go for days at a stretch in the saddle, good trackers and trailers, and all were handy with a rifle and six-gun. Bill Doolin was truly one of them.

BIBLIOGRAPHY

Books

Adams, Ramon F. *Burs Under the Saddle*. Norman, University of Oklahoma Press, 1964.

———. *Six-Guns and Saddle Leather*. Norman, University of Oklahoma Press, 1954.

Barnard, Evan G. *A Rider of the Cherokee Strip*. Boston, Houghton Mifflin Co., 1936.

Bartholomew, Ed. *Biographical Album of Western Gunfighters*. Houston, Frontier Press of Texas, 1958.

Canton, Frank. *Frontier Trails*. Boston, Houghton Mifflin Co., 1930.

Croy, Homer. *He Hanged Them High*. New York, Duell, Sloan & Pearce, 1956.

———. *Trigger Marshal*. New York, Duell, Sloan & Pearce, 1958.

Dalton, Emmett. *When the Daltons Rode*. New York, Doubleday, Doran & Co., 1931.

———. *The Dalton Brothers*. New York, Frederick Fell, Inc., 1954.

Day, B. F. *Gene Rhodes, Cowboy*. New York, Julian Messner, Inc., 1954.

Gish, Anthony. *American Bandits*. Girard, Kan., Halderman-Julius Publications, 1938.

Graves, Richard S. *Oklahoma Outlaw*. Oklahoma City, State Printing and Publishing Co., 1915.

Halsell, H. H. *The Old Cimarron*, Lubbock, Tex., privately printed.

———. *Cowboys and Cattleland*. Dallas, Wilkinson Printing Co., n.d.

Harmon, S. W. *Hell on the Border*. Fort Smith, Phoenix Publishing Co., 1898.

Hendricks, George D. *The Bad-Man of the West*. San Antonio, Naylor Co., 1941.

Horan, James D., and Paul Sann. *Pictorial History of the Wild West*. New York, Crown Publishers, Inc., 1954.

Hunter, Marvin J., and Noah H. Rose. *The Album of Gunfighters*. Houston, Warren Hunter, 1959.

McDonald, A. B. *Hands Up*. Indianapolis, Bobbs-Merrill Co., 1927.

McGinty, Bill. *The Old West*. Ripley, Okla., Ripley Review Publishers, n.d.

Masterson, W. B. (Bat). *Famous Gunfighters of the Western Frontier*. Ruidoso, N.M., Frontier Book Co., 1959.

Miller, Nyle H., and Joseph W. Snell. *Why The West Was Wild*. Topeka, Kansas State Historical Society, 1963.

Newsom, J. A. *The Life and Practices of the Wild and Modern Indian*. Oklahoma City, Harlow Publishing Co., 1923.

Nix, Evett Dumas. *Oklahombres*. St. Louis, Eden Publishing House, 1929.

Preece, Harold. *The Dalton Gang*. New York, Hastings House, 1963.

Raine, William MacLeod. *Famous Sheriffs and Outlaws*. Garden City, N.Y., Doubleday, Doran & Co., 1929.

Rainey, George. *The Cherokee Strip*. Guthrie, Okla., Cooperative Publishing Co., 1933.

Rhodes, May Davison. *The Hired Man on Horse Back*. Boston, Houghton Mifflin Co., 1938.

Rouse, M. C. *A History of Cowboy Flat-Campbell-Pleasant Valley*. Guthrie, Okla., privately printed, 1960.

Ruth, Kent, *et al*. *Oklahoma: A Guide to the Sooner State*. Norman, University of Oklahoma Press, 1958.

Shackleford, William Yancey. *Gun-fighters of the Old West*. Girard, Kan., Halderman-Julius Publications, 1943.

Shirk, George II. *Oklahoma Place-Names*. Norman, University of Oklahoma Press, 1965.

Shirley, Glenn. *Heck Thomas, Frontier Marshal*. Philadelphia, Chilton Co., 1962.

———. *Law West of Fort Smith*. New York, Henry Holt and Co., 1957.

———. *Six-Gun and Silver Star*. Albuquerque, University of New Mexico Press, 1955.

———. *Toughest of Them All*. Albuquerque, University of New Mexico Press, 1953.

Tilghman, Zoe A. *Marshal of the Last Frontier*. Glendale, Calif., Arthur H. Clark Co., 1949.

———. *Outlaw Days*. Oklahoma City, Harlow Publishing Co., 1926.

Wellman, Paul I. *A Dynasty of Western Outlaws*. New York, Doubleday, 1961.

Articles

"Indian Pioneer History" (Foreman Collection, Vols. 1–113). Oklahoma Historical Society.

Williams, Jim. "Indian Pioneer History." Oklahoma Historical Society.

Documents

Doolin, John. Military Record (Photocopies)

Doolin, William. Coroner's Inquest, U.S. vs. William Doolin, August 27, 1896.

Record of Interments, Summit View Cemetery, Logan County, O. T., 1895–1896.

Interviews

Hoke, Harry, by Author, Jan. 15, 1961.

McCubbin, Cliff, by Author, July 31, 1962.

Shirley, Glenn, by Author, July 12, 1961.

Traband, Phil, by Author, March 16, 1960.

Letters

Bowles, Frances M., to Author, Jan. 11, 1960; June 14, 1960; Apr. 12, 1961; May 2, 1961.

Clark, Nora T., to Author, Dec. 2, 1960; Apr. 22, 1961.

Ellsworth, I. L., to Author, Sept. 28, 1961.

Fraker, Elmer L., to Author, Aug. 21, 1961.

Hoke, Harry, to Author, Dec. 17, 1962.

Holmes, Kenneth B., to Author, May 5, 1960; Jan. 25, 1961.

Jarvis, Rose I. (Court Clerk, Payne County, Oklahoma), to Author, July 13, 1961.

Lewis, Frances, to Author, March 18, 1961.

McGinty, Clarence, to Author, March 17, 1961.

McRill, Leslie A., to Author, Feb. 8, 1961.

Madsen, C. R., to Author, May 7, 1960.

May, A. D., to Author, March 27, 1961.

Meek, Jay Doolin, to Author, Apr. 28, 1960; June 7, 1960; May 2, 1961.

Meeks, Beth Thomas, to Author, Feb. 2, 1960; Apr. 4, 1960; May 19, 1960.

Melton, John H., to Roy P. Stewart, Aug. 25, 1962.

Osborn, Al (Shy), to Author, March 24, 1961.

Payne County Court Clerk to Author, Jan. 26, 1961; Aug. 29, 1961.

Ramey, W. T., to Author, June 18, 1962.

Rhodes, Alan, to Author, Aug. 5, 1960; Aug. 21, 1960.

Selph, E. J., to Author, March 19, 1961.

Tilghman, Zoe A., to Author, Jan. 19, 1961; June 3, 1961.

Wetzel, Guy (Postmaster, Longview, Texas), to Author, Feb. 20, 1961.

Newspapers

Beaver Herald, Beaver, O. T., Jan. 2, 1896.

Burden Times, Burden, Kan., Dec. 11, 1947.

O'Collegian, Oklahoma A&M College, Stillwater, Okla., May 2, 1926.

Caney Chronicle, Caney, Kan., Oct. 14, 1892.

Carthage Press, Carthage, Mo., May 17, 1894.

Cassville Republican, Cassville, Mo., May 17, 1894.

Daily Ardmoreite, Ardmore, O. T., Sept. 6, 1894; Sept. 28, 1894.

Daily Capitol, Topeka, Kan., June 11, 1893.

Daily Oklahoman, Oklahoma City, Okla., Feb. 20, 1894; June 5, 1894; Sept. 19, 1894; May 3, 1896; Aug. 25, 1896; Aug. 29, 1896; June 13, 1915; May 8, 1921; July 14, 1937; Sept. 4, 1960; Nov. 13, 1961; Aug. 28, 1962; Oct. 27, 1963.

Edmond Sun-Democrat, Edmond, O. T., June 29, 1894; Sept. 14, 1894; Jan. 24, 1896; Jan. 29, 1896; Jan. 31, 1896; July 21, 1896; July 23, 1896; Aug. 7, 1896; March 5, 1897.

Elevator, Topeka, Kan., May 15, 1891.

El Reno News, El Reno, O. T., June 24, 1896; July 3, 1896; July 10, 1896; July 24, 1896; Aug. 7, 1896; Sept. 4, 1896; Sept. 11, 1896; Sept. 18, 1896; Nov. 20, 1896; March 5, 1897.

Evening Gazette, Oklahoma City, O. T., Nov. 9, 1892.

Globe Republican, Dodge City, Kan., Nov. 4, 1892.

Guthrie Daily Leader, Guthrie, Okla., Apr. 11, 1896; June 20, 1896; July 2, 1896; Nov. 8, 1896; Sept. 6, 1959; Apr. 17, 1960; Apr. 14, 1963; July 22, 1963.

Kingfisher Free Press, Kingfisher, O. T., Jan. 2, 1896; Jan. 30, 1896; March 4, 1897.

Lamar Democrat, Lamar, Mo., May 17, 1894.

Lawrence Chieftain, Mt. Vernon, Mo., May 17, 1894.

Los Angeles Times, Los Angeles, Calif., March 29, 1953.

Miner and Mechanic, Neosho, Mo., May 12, 1894; May 30, 1894.

Oklahoma Journal, Oklahoma City, O. T., Nov. 9, 1892.

Oklahoman's Orbit, Oklahoma City, Okla., Sept. 27, 1959; Jan. 3, 1960; Jan. 10, 1960; May 7, 1961; Oct. 22, 1961.

Oklahoma State Capital, Guthrie, O. T., May 8, 1891; June 12, 1893; Oct. 13, 1893; Apr. 1, 1899.

Ponca City News, Ponca City, Okla., Apr. 25, 1960.

Bibliography

St. Louis Republic, St. Louis, Mo., May 11, 1894.

Southwest City Enterprise, Southwest City, Mo., May 11, 1894.

Stillwater Gazette, Stillwater, O. T., Nov. 11, 1892; Aug. 8, 1895; Jan. 16, 1896; Jan. 23, 1896; Jan. 30, 1896; Aug. 27, 1896; Nov. 12, 1896; Nov. 22, 1900.

Stillwater News-Press, Stillwater, Okla., March 2, 1960.

Vinita Leader, Vinita, O. T., July 3, 1896; Sept. 17, 1896.

Miscellaneous

American Heritage, August, 1960.

City of Guthrie Directory, Guthrie, O. T., 1894, 1896, 1897.

Chronicles of Oklahoma, Vol. XXX (1952); Winter, 1958–59.

Golden West, January, 1966.

Guns, March, 1963.

Gun Report, February, 1957.

Oklahoma Ranch and Farm World, Aug. 9, 1959.

One Hundred Years of History and Progress, 1849–1949, Centennial Edition of McDonald County, Missouri.

Saga, October, 1960.

Santa Fe Magazine, April, May, June, 1955.

True West, September, 1954; January–February, 1956; May–June, 1960; July–August, 1962; February, 1966.

Index

DISCARDED